**The Stuff You Can't Bottle:
Advertising for
the Global Youth Market**

By King Adz

**With 275 illustrations,
250 in colour**

Thames & Hudson

**For Jamie Camplin
– the Original G.**

First published in the United
Kingdom in 2013 by Thames &
Hudson Ltd, 181A High Holborn,
London WC1V 7QX

Design and layout by INT Works

British Library Cataloguing-in-
Publication Data

A catalogue record for this book is
available from the British Library

ISBN 978-0-500-29075-0

Printed and bound in China
by C&C Offset Printing Co. Ltd.

To find out about all our
publications, please visit
www.thamesandhudson.com.
There you can subscribe to our
e-newsletter, browse or download
our current catalogue, and buy any
titles that are in print.

Contents

Contents

Contents

01 ⁸

How do you capture something so dynamic, so fleeting, that it's gone before you know it? Where does this quality come from? Who really knows what can make a connection with the youth? This is a journey into the lives of the free and the domain of the restless – a place where the true spirit of liberty and energy of the young bounce off every surface and run rings around anyone over the age of 24. It may seem a fruitless, impossible quest, but I hope to capture some of the stuff you can't bottle.... Let me take you down.

01 ⁹ **88 ways into the minds of youth: Begin here**

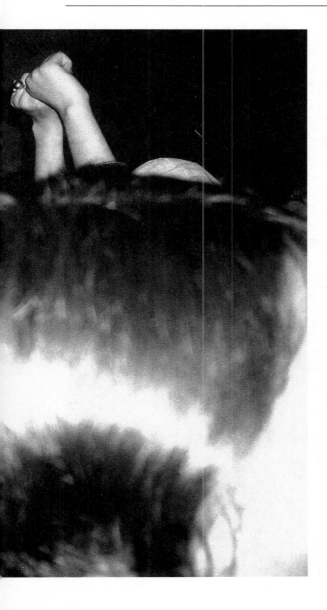

02

My starting point is advertising taken in its broadest sense: the communication of various concepts to the youth demographic, using any of the available media, ultimately with a view to selling a product. The core of any successful creative venture lies in the story – the idea, whether big or small – that draws you in. This book is a document of my journey through some of those ideas, examining the art, images, words and concepts that are needed to convey these messages successfully to a mass audience. I interviewed many different talents and legends in the advertising industry and beyond. Each inspired me to broaden my view – and this is when it became interesting.

One of the most profound effects of the digital revolution is the radical change it has had on the delivery of advertising, propelling it from the traditional meat and two veg (TV and print) into a multifaceted, multimedia, multi-sensory experience. And youth advertising (communications aimed at 16- to 24-year-olds) is already way ahead in the future – this is often where the most exciting, progressive ideas and concepts get through and make it into production. It is a truly mind-blowing creative "arena", where the message is often the medium and the medium changes so rapidly that only the very savvy can keep up. That is, unless you're young, and then it's just second nature; you get it all in the blink of an eye and you're on to the next big thing, taking

"We used to start with commerce and work out to the culture, and now we need to start with culture and work back to commerce."

"The Internet has changed the game totally and utterly, yet not at all. In other words, despite everything, an idea is the one element that is key. The idea is still everything and it needs to carry everything else. A good idea will always win out. Bad ideas still sink without a trace. Everything else is just about mechanics, delivery, amplification and how people get to engage with the idea."

Nike China by Wieden+Kennedy Shanghai.

it in your stride and hungry for more. But, saying that, the one vital ingredient is still a great idea. Without this, the communication – however it's packaged – will disappear very quickly indeed.

One point I must make here is that although the youth demographic is traditionally defined as 16 to 24, in reality it's more like 14 to 44; the parameters of this market seem to keep changing at both ends. The days of people settling down at 25 are long gone, and kids grow up faster and faster. It is also worth pointing out that the whole youth "thing" is a bit of a conundrum: no one really knows why anything works (when it does), but it is always painfully obvious when something fails. This uncertainty makes it a much more

exciting subject to be documenting and, I hope, getting across in this book.

The second real revolution in advertising (the first was when Bill Bernbach moved the copywriter and art director into the same room) was the coming of age of the TV spot in the 1970s, when it took over as the number one media choice for advertisers, which in turn had an effect on how print ads were created and produced. Advertising is part of a circle of evolution: one thing influences another, and vice versa. This is also what happened in the 1990s and 2000s: the digital revolution created the need for something tactile, something analogue, and together they produced a very exciting and progressive method of communication, best

02   12   **Introduction:**   ↓ **Erik Kessels. Creative Director and**
         The stuff you can't bottle...   **co-founder, KesselsKramer**
                                            ↓ **George Lois. Ad legend**

"The difficulty with describing the effectiveness of youth advertising is that the category is hard to define. Perhaps this is because 'youth' means very little now: 35-year-olds still go to gigs, still play computer games, still go clubbing, marry later, have kids later. The genius of PlayStation commercials is that they recognize this. They are targeted at mid-thirties men as much as they are at boys."

"My kind of advertising has a big idea that's sharp. I don't talk to people like they're young or old, I talk to smart people. The problem with most people's ideas in advertising is that they don't think people are smart. They think the youth won't get it. Bullshit! People are smart as hell and TV and advertising are part of their culture. People are smart whether they're young, middle-aged or old. If you think the youth won't get your idea then you wind up with uncommunicative advertising, and if you think people are dumb then you're gonna do dumb advertising."

seen on a mobile platform/smartphone roaming through a city, with the virtual influencing the real. But behind this you still need that original idea. The BIG IDEA.

Youth advertising is often taken care of by the regular mainstream advertising agencies, though there are a few specialist firms that solely look after the youth demographic. OK, so I'm probably opening a can of worms here, but even the agencies that brand themselves as "youth specialists" are no more clued-up than the larger ones. This is not because they don't care or do good work – it's more down to the fact that if you spend your days working in an agency on advertising campaigns, you are not out there on

the street looking at what the youth are doing, what they are into, what's getting them going. There are lots of youth research and "insight" agencies, but they don't really have much more of a clue; the information they are looking for isn't something you can quantify or sum up in a report sheet, or discover through data patterns, or glean through research. You can track what the youth were buying yesterday, but you can't predict what they're going to be into next month as they don't even know themselves.

Youth advertising is something very specialist. Its energy and raison d'être make it unlike mainstream advertising. It is a totally unique proposition that demands a different approach.

02   13   **Introduction:**
The stuff you can't bottle...   ↓   **Chris Colborn. Executive VP Chief**
Experience Officer, R/GA

"It's more about marketing than advertising; it's not necessarily about buying clicks, or views, or anything else. It's about engaging with your consumer in a way that's meaningful and relevant. More often than not there is a shift – especially among youth – towards owned-media generating earned-media to make the real connection, versus the old pay-media metaphor where advertising had a payday. There is still relevance and value for traditional hop-on advertising, but the inevitable shift is towards this balance where you're engaging with your consumer across multiple channels. The social revolution is more of a popular revolution, people taking charge of their conversation and interests – like paying with a tweet. The people have spoken and brands and businesses must adapt. There are still great opportunities for brands in this changing landscape, but if they fail to adapt they will suffer the consequences."

The idea for this book is not only to explore the past, present and future of youth advertising and communication, but also to show exactly why certain groundbreaking pieces worked, and, using these clues, look to the future to see where we are going.

Just as I started writing this book, I got a call from someone working at a well-known agency who had a meeting with a very youthful Italian fashion brand and, having heard that I'd recently worked with this brand, wanted my input. She admitted she was middle-aged and knew nothing about what was "cool" these days, and therefore had no connection with the youth. She was going to talk to the brand about doing some work aimed at the female market, and wanted to know my thoughts. It was a slightly surreal moment. This backs up what I said: people who work in ad agencies don't have the connection to what the youth of the world are into, and, unfortunately, this isn't something you can Google. The one thing you need is a connection (to the consumer, to the brand, to something real), otherwise it won't work – it will be just background noise, and there is already too much of that around.

I've been in and out of advertising since the early 1990s, and no matter how often I try to get some distance between us, I'm somehow always drawn back in. Steve Henry (who we'll hear from later) reckons that advertising is the place where life's

"I believe brands are becoming much more personal. We're creating virtual bonfires; we're throwing logs on those bonfires and inviting our customers to sit with us around those fires and tell our story. And if you've got a good story then people will listen, and if it's boring then they're not going to. That's the market, that's the Internet. Give me your story. You're as good as the energy you give out. It's who you are, and that's what people are seeking – authenticity, genuine stories. We're all looking for someone who's going to share something genuine with me that I love and that makes me laugh and get up and slam the table and sink another beer. But that requires courage; it requires the willingness to fail, the absence of fear – in other words, love. It requires that people love their customer and it requires that they remove the illusion of separation. We are not separate from our customers, we are all part of the whole. People mistakenly think it's about branding

misfits end up, which in my case is true – who says they want to be in advertising when they are a kid? Back in the 1990s, when I worked full-time in an agency, I would do what I thought was my best possible work, only to be told (by the client, by the agency) that it was too "edgy" and have the work rejected. Today, this "edge" is one of the vital ingredients that brands desperately need in their advertising to engage the youth market, and it is fortunate that this is what I live breathe eat sleep think dream. The only way to connect is to speak their language (audio and visual). Youth. Edge. Engage. It took me a while, but I eventually recognized that this was my demographic – although I'm not sure how long I can make this last! If advertising is full of misfits,

then youth advertising is a place for proper social outcasts, the creative mentalists. For this book I have travelled the world and tried to get as close as possible to the creation of some cutting-edge youth advertising, and then report back from the front line.

P.S. By the time this book hits the shelf, the youth will be into/onto something else.

P.P.S. Just as I was putting this book to bed, Felix Baumgartner fell to earth from the edge of space, in a glorious piece of content creation for Red Bull. Who would have thought that this would be seen as one of the greatest pieces of youth advertising ever?

and messaging. It's all about who you really are. They will sniff you out, and if you are not telling the truth then they will drop you like a bad habit."

**Light drawing by
LICHTFAKTOR for dENiZEN.**

03

As I mentioned in the Introduction, advertising – youth advertising in particular – has been transformed by the new media. My purpose in this book is to define what it has become, and then to ask what it should become to be properly effective and, perhaps more importantly, a truly creative platform on which amazing work can be produced. To understand this we have to know where we are, and how we got here.

Word of mouth was once the king of all advertising. If you could somehow generate just a little chatter, or "buzz", as it is often referred to, then your brand "fire" would be well and truly ignited and you'd get some of that all-important "heat". But that's changed. Now you need a combination of word of mouth (both analogue – in the real world – and digital), plus some user input and testing of the product, plus some entertainment-esque content to show you care or know what you're talking about. If you're lucky, this might translate into a sale, although more often these days consumers like to get it for free if they possibly can. This is one of the biggest problems facing brands, and one of the oldest conundrums out there: how do you actually separate the youth from their money?

As in the film industry, there are no tried-and-tested formulas for advertising success: no one really knows what they're talking about. There are no absolutes. Back in the 1980s, the music

03   17   **Where youth advertising is right now**

↓ **Banksy. Ex-advertising executive**
↓ **John Hunt. Worldwide Creative Director, TBWA\Worldwide**

"The thing I hate the most about advertising is that it attracts all the bright, creative and ambitious young people, leaving us mainly with the slow and self-obsessed to become our artists. Modern art is a disaster area. Never in the field of human history has so much been used by so many to say so little."

"In the broad philosophical sense, I think word of mouth is still paramount. There is nothing more important than a mate, a peer – someone whose point of view you hold in high regard – saying either this ad or this product or this event is great, because that carries all the ballast. It's an opinion with some credibility versus just reading it on- or offline. The flip side is that some people think if you get two million hits in four days, the job is done. Often the youth consume media in just a nanosecond, so it's quite tricky to get stickiness."

industry was initially against the idea of MTV, as they thought it would damage record sales. They believed it would kill the business. How wrong can you be? It's a bit like thinking that the digital revolution (advertising's equivalent of the Industrial Revolution) is harmful to our industry, when we all know that this is what's going to take advertising to the next level, and this is the moment we have all been waiting for. Advertising now has the potential to become something truly great; we just need to get rid of a few dinosaurs standing in our way.

Digital advances have forced advertising as a whole to move from broad- to narrow-casting; thanks to social networking and other online communication tools, the one-way stream of information (billboard, TV or print ads) has become a two-way highway of valuable information, for both consumer and brand. So, with this in mind, the only two questions you need to ask of any communication are: "What's your point?" and "Why should I care?" If those questions are answered with a narrative that's involving, inspiring and interesting, then you've got something – and if they're not, then you need to think harder, as all you really have is a product that sits on a shelf. Saying nothing.

It's a bit like dinner-party chat. If you sit next to someone interesting and entertaining, then your night is great. If that person is a self-centred bore

---

03   18   **Where youth advertising is right now**   ↓ **Sefi Shaked. CD, IMSADV, Tel Aviv**
↓ **Victoria Nyberg. Strategist, Naked Communications**

"At first, the Internet was an unknown territory, which enabled the optimization geeks to use the lack of knowledge among advertisers to take control of that media. What we got was a boring world of banners. When the social networks finally arrived, it became interesting. A great idea is something that people love to share – and that turned us, classic advertising people, on! Finally, the power is not only in the hands of the brands, but also in the hands of consumers – and that duet is really interesting. Today, the big idea rules again and the Internet media buyers are back in their natural habitat of…buying banners. The real advertising people are celebrating the social networks and achieving a very strong engagement for their brands."

"I think that brands can play a bigger and more meaningful role in people's lives by sharing passions and enemies. If you mix that with exciting and interactive storytelling, brands could

and only drivels on about themselves, it's going to be a crap night and you'll want to switch places – or go home. This is the basis of all great youth communication: telling a story properly, telling the right story in the right way to the right audience and, much more importantly, listening to what the other person (the target market, the subculture) has to say, preferably right at the beginning. Mix this with some content-enhancing technology and then you're rolling – you can create something that is authentic, engaging and relevant to the brand and its customers.

But, ultimately, however much we talk about "making a connection" or "creating a relationship", advertising is all about selling. There is no way around this. Without sales none of us would be here. We'd have to get proper jobs! And it all goes back to that well-used advertising phrase: the art of separating people from their money is why advertising exists. This is the bottom line.

engage young consumers beyond their wildest dreams. Today, gamification is everywhere, and we all are wired to love games. Personally, I think that small is going to be the new BIG!! Why? Because there is no way a brand can do everything. Brands have to become more niche to really engage and get under the skin of the younger generation."

"One of the things we are wrestling with is that all the basic marketing tools of the 20th century, for media and brand promotion, don't work like they used to. We have a huge market in which people are looking to each other as opposed to the media for trends; things bubble up from the streets rather than being pushed down from the media ether. One of the problems is that advertising is controlled by people in their late twenties and early thirties who either want to talk to each other or want to talk to youth. They don't want to talk to people who are older than they are."

04

Word of mouth was the old-school version of social networking, and this is one thing that is still essential if you are selling to the youth. They listen to their own; they listen to peers ("early adopters") whom they consider cool. This was demonstrated perfectly by the skate, surf and street brand Stüssy.

For today's brands, using social networking to sell their products is nothing new. There are plenty of people talking about how their advertising can be a two-way conversation between brand and customer, and we've seen how platforms like Facebook and Twitter have upped the game, but if you want to know the future you have to check the past, and this is where one of the greatest-ever youth brands comes into it. Which is a great place to start.

Back in the late 1980s, Shawn Stüssy created one of the freshest clothing labels around, and then used social events to get word on the streets – literally – which then spread across the world. Originally a surfboard shaper by trade, Shawn realized that he could only produce one board a day, and so began to screen-print his signature onto T-shirts to supplement his income. By the mid-1980s he was selling his clothes in the hippest New York skate- and street-wear shops, and had begun to build up an international network of like-minded people, which he then branded the International Stüssy Tribe: an organic crew who

"Shaping was something I could not mess with or whore out. Board shaping was sculpting in the purest form to me. Magic boards were just that – born out of the creative process. It might sound corny, but this shit mattered to me. The T-shirt thing made sense. I could goof around with the design, pass it on to someone else for production, then ship it myself. This situation let me continue to shape boards while developing the clothing part of it.

The tribe was not a countable deal, just friends coming together through like-minded stuff. The parties were loose BBQ affairs at the beginning – later they became bigger. The party at Gold in Tokyo was the zenith of the genre, around 1990–91.

Each advert was a full page, black and white, run in either a skate or surf mag, usually done around midnight till 2 a.m. the night before it was due for

sported custom-made personalized track jackets and had bundles of tongue-in-cheek flavour to spare.

His fresh-to-death brand of clothing, influenced by skaters, surfers and artists, including tribal artists (especially African), reggae musicians and hip-hop DJs, kept selling and built a very loyal following around the world. By the end of the 1980s his small company had become a global street brand.

Stüssy's success came down to several factors. The brand was born out of necessity, and evolved organically. It had a strong look (the logo was tight!) and impeccable influences. Shawn spread the word

by throwing parties in the coolest cities (LA, New York, London, Tokyo) and from these it extended outwards, as the youth all wanted to be part of what was happening; part of the Stüssy tribe.

printing. Always fast, X-Acto-blade rough cut-out felt-pen lettering. 'Don't think too much,' I would say to myself, turn up the music, get herbal and put out some shit – that was my style. It's kinda weird that all these years later a corporation can still drive its engine with the same goods. It was all done with a punk ethic, fuck those existing surf companies, panty-waist posers. It was never meant to stand the test of time, and for that I am proud – when stuff is supposed to happen, it will, but only when the work is a real part of your life, not because you are 'creating a brand', do you follow me?"

First and last! More than thirty years of Stüssy advertising, side by side.

05

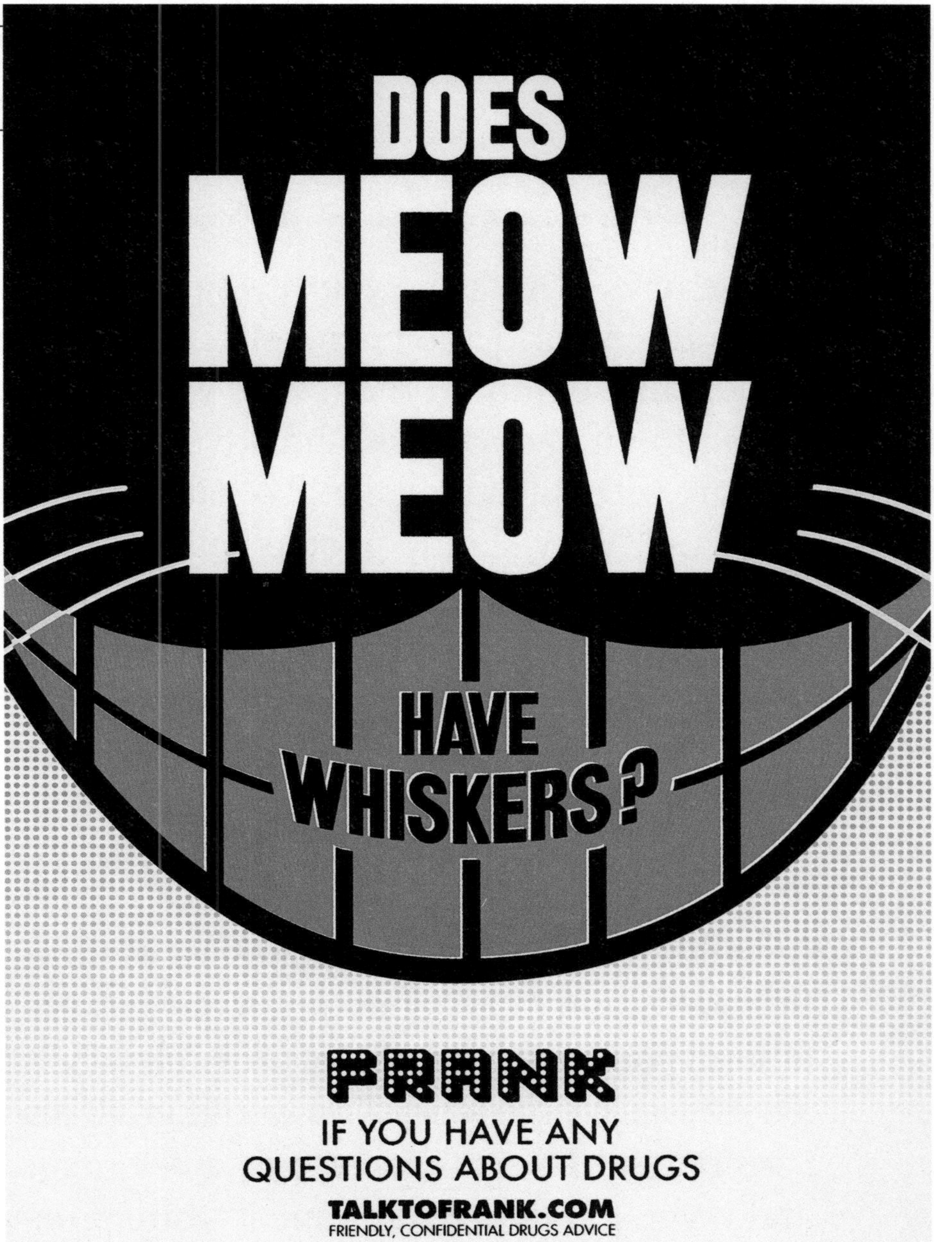

DOES **MEOW MEOW** HAVE WHISKERS?

FRANK
IF YOU HAVE ANY
QUESTIONS ABOUT DRUGS
TALKTOFRANK.COM
FRIENDLY, CONFIDENTIAL DRUGS ADVICE

Mother has always had an unparalleled youthful and rebellious attitude, which is great when you're the world's largest independent advertising agency with the following philosophy: "To make great work, have fun and make money. Always in that order" – which I'm sure is part of the secret of its success. I was fortunate enough to spend some time with Dylan Williams, Mother's chief strategy officer – a fellow Casual and lover of the street. We took a stroll around London's East End and talked about the business.

How do you separate the youth from their money?

"These days I think the youth want brands to hang out in their world and positively contribute to it, rather than bombard them with whatever they're trying to unload. Brands and advertisers used to start with questions like: 'What are we gonna say?' and 'Why should people believe this?' but today it's more like: 'What culture or subculture are we gonna be part of?' and 'What might we credibly do to contribute to the surroundings, and be rewarded commercially and culturally?'"

Advertising imagery, as a whole, is all becoming rather homogenized. How is the youth work different?

"It could well be that advertising, as we have come to understand it, is not going to be very effective among young people, so we probably won't do it. There was a time when you would go to one of two commercial TV stations or only a few magazines, and if you got in the right one it would guarantee

Mother's launch for American retailer Target – using the Standard Hotel in New York as a stage/screen.

you an audience of the right opinion-leading kids and early adopters, and you'd be likely to hit one in three. I don't think this adds up any more.

Before, there weren't that many different channels that emerging photographers, fashion designers or artists could use to get their shit out there. More often than not, they had to wrap it around a commercial message to give force to what they were about creatively. These days you don't need to hang out with Beck's beer to get your art/fashion/music out into the world; there are lots of other ways in which you can make your creativity have an effect without needing to peg yourself to Coca-Cola or Levi's or Nike. You used to read about Tracey Emin and how she got her first break with Beck's, or some of the early promo directors, saying, 'If it wasn't for Wrangler jeans no one would ever have heard of me,' but these days talent doesn't need to take on advertising jobs in order to reach young people.

...or the dog gets it! Frank anti-drugs commercial.

There are lots of other ways of doing it. That said, it doesn't mean that brands can't connect with young people, or positively contribute to their cultures. Brands like Red Bull and Converse are doing some interesting stuff, and it's not what you'd call a conventional thirty-second TV spot or a DPS. It's not anything remotely corporate either. The thinking is, 'How can I help young people – they need a place to hang out and play music.'"

**Do you think the youth's perception
of advertising has changed?**

"Advertising has become a kind of wallpaper for their culture. I don't think there is any anger or resentment towards it – they're really quite ambivalent. They shrug their shoulders and don't really notice much of it, and then occasionally something will tickle their fancy. Most of it is laughed at, as they find it boring. I think the bigger concern for advertisers, or

Curiosity killed the dog. Frank anti-drugs commercial.

big companies that use advertising, is the fact that advertising is failing to interrupt young people at all now."

The biggest mistake is when you make something that the youth are ambivalent about.

"Take Oliviero Toscani's work for Benetton, which looked to upset 85 per cent of people when it originally came out – these days you are not going to upset the kids. They can see some horrendous shit online, so what the fuck are we going to put on a forty-eight-sheet poster that's going to shock this lot? Nothing at all! The big companies are increasingly risk-averse so they put all their communication through the same strategic wind tunnel, which results in increasingly similar work being produced. It all just blends in and kids won't be the slightest bit interested in it. So by being risk-averse they are becoming more ineffective as companies, which is crazy. But at a certain point in time someone smart is going to realize that

this is the issue and start taking risks, and I think young people are going to applaud that, as they are all media-savvy and literate enough to know that a big brand doing something semi-brave is worthy of applause. It's harder to do something real if you're Coke.

In many ways some of the best advertising I've seen for young people has been product design. Gel in trainers, a waffle sole, or stuff like Nike Chat – where they get the trainer obsessives to talk to their designers. They ask them stuff like, 'What would you do with the Air Max X?' or 'Shall we do the deal with Apple?' And this begins to make the consumer feel like they are a part of the company."

IS SKUNK STRONGER THAN BADGER?

FRANK
IF YOU HAVE ANY
QUESTIONS ABOUT DRUGS
TALKTOFRANK.COM
FRIENDLY, CONFIDENTIAL DRUGS ADVICE

Questions that need answering by Frank.

How do you stay up in the game?

"I'm knocking 40 and I don't go out as much as I used to. The most important thing for Mother as a company – our single source of competitive difference – is our cultural sensitivity. And the way we stay culturally sensitive is through the right recruitment; we hire the right people. We watch them arrive and we can spot almost before they come in if they've got the spark, if they dress a little bit different. And most of the time we get it right, but when we get it wrong we spectacularly fail. We try to hire interesting people to work with full time, and we try to hang out with people who we might be able to help, and who might be able to help us, and we become part of an ecosystem – for want of a better word – where we all help each other."

06

The R-word can often be a dirty word in creative circles, and in the traditional sense – a client demanding a great idea to be tested, tested and then tested again; or the traditional and thoroughly crap "focus group" – it is, especially when applied to the youth market. But with the new model of advertising (the stuff you can't bottle), research is an essential part of the process, and is vital for an understanding of both the market and the product – but only if it's done with a completely open, honest method that includes the youth from the get-go.

Certain products (especially films and TV) are now initially developed with the purchase of some seemingly random Google AdWords.

These are linked to a dead site with a simple holding page, which is monitored, and the most popular word (with the most clicks) is then developed into some form of entertainment (books, TV, films). As insane as this sounds, it is happening right now. The process does get more and more complex as it progresses, as the data from the public reaction to the concept is fed back into the project and controls the path of the narrative as it moves forward. It's almost like a live focus group. For some forms of mainstream entertainment, this is how content is going to be created: the risk is reduced by user-testing the concept while it's in development before going ahead and spending millions on a brand and then millions on promotion. This is relevant to

---

"The best research is walking the streets, going to festivals, and social media."

"Advertisers won't do anything any more without us doing research first. And they do the research in a really surreptitious, back-alley kind of way: typically an ex-primary school teacher hosts focus groups in suburbia and asks stupid questions to people who turn up to get paid £50 and take the piss with their answers. This data gets fed back into some enormous company that makes huge creative decisions on the back of it. Instead, if you were to make the research part of the equation and ask people publicly what they would do, this would be so much more productive. New Coke? Yes or no? The drinks group Diageo did this when they signed up Puff Daddy to help sell their drinks. Slowly but surely that worked. What would be even smarter is if you asked whether it should be Puff Daddy, or Odd Future?"

advertising, because the product and creative can be tested online with virtual research rooms before the launch. However, I'm not sure how effective all this is compared with actually getting out there and talking to the youth; this is when they will be straight up with you. I've spent a lot of time on the street making connections, which is when I've done all my relevant research and documentation. It has become a big part of my working life – almost more important than the actual creative.

Research for youth advertising works well when it's relevant to solving a business problem. It is not about finding out what the consumer's favourite colour, or tune, or sneaker is, and then creating something in those colours, or using that sound or style. It's about proving or disproving theories and creative solutions about what a brand should do to become more successful, and what's currently stopping this from happening.

I recently advised a skate-wear brand who wanted to discover exactly how they could step up their game and become a global lifestyle brand. I suggested that, rather than hiring a large and well-known corporate research firm (which was very good at what it did), they should start on the ground level and run events and workshops at skate parks, music festivals, street-art events and beach sports tournaments, etc., to find out what

"I don't use the term 'research' lightly. Anthropology and behavioural research are where you find the very, very interesting and creative people who work in that space and who understand people and behaviour. They bring some really powerful insights."

Stencil from Berlin. The youth have spoken.

the 16- to 24-year-olds thought about the brand, and how they thought the brand could take it to the next level. Obviously I didn't suggest that they actually ask the kids those questions directly, but the data would certainly flow and, because of the unorthodox methods, it would be authentic.

If you put young people in a research environment (i.e. anywhere other than their usual habitat or hang-out) then they will behave in a different way and the data will not be accurate. You have to talk to them in their own hood, on their terms, and ideally in their language. Admittedly, this is almost impossible, as by the time the brand, the agency, etc., have signed off the job, the language and ideas will have become dated and the moment will have passed. Research has to be spontaneous and authentic – only then will you get something that will help propel the brand forward.

---

06   ³³   **Research**   ↓   **Susanna Glenndahl Thorslund.**
Client Service Director, CP+B Europe

"Research always works well. Researching how a haulage contractor purchases trucks in different markets may seem to require a larger effort than looking into how chocolate bars are consumed in Sweden – for the simple reason that the advertising team itself has bought many chocolate bars in Sweden. But in fact, there is no real difference – you always need a deep understanding of decision-making processes, purchase processes, target groups, and what category-related truths you need to challenge to be able to do really strong advertising."

07

When I unpacked my car I was surprised and confused by what I found. How did that Digimon get there?

Intel created an ingenious research programme in which they got people around the world to unpack their cars. This gave the researchers a unique insight into those people's lives, and helped them understand how their behaviour was going to change, where it was going – and what products Intel should be developing. This kind of field research – what I would call proper research – works amazingly well. You have to go out to people, rather than bringing them into a sterile environment and showing them some product you're developing while feeding them beer and crisps.

"I think research works best when you let the data speak, when you can find a way to have the object of the research tell you things you didn't expect. I love being surprised by research. So why are we unpacking cars? And what might it yield? And why is it anthropological? And why might we be doing this for Intel?"

"There are more than eight hundred million cars currently on the world's roads, representing a significant investment of resources, from the cost of purchasing and maintaining a passenger vehicle to the larger fiscal demand of building and maintaining road infrastructure. Furthermore, cars are a significant site of human activity. We wanted to see cars with fresh eyes, and to think about them as a field site in and of themselves; in short, as an object of study. We started with some very simple questions: what is a car, what does it mean to own a car, to use one, to care for one? Armed with a very basic set of tools: a tarp (a shower curtain, really), a folding step-stool and cameras, we set off to interview car owners and users in the US, the UK, Australia, Singapore, China, Malaysia and Brazil. We wanted to see what people carried with them and to help make sense of the ways in which cars functioned as sites of technology consumption and of human activity and meaning-making. And we have been unpacking cars ever since.

In all our excavations, it quickly became clear that cars are always sites of personal technology consumption – phones, Bluetooth headsets, music players, mapping systems, portable DVD players, etc. Cars function as sites in which a great deal of technology rests – some of it is built into the vehicle (in-vehicle information and navigation systems), some of it is brought to the car daily and leaves again (mobile phones and laptops), and some technology has found its way into the car and has never left (chargers, SIM cards, digital music players, navigation systems). This means cars are full of cables, plugs, batteries and after-market hacks and modifications to make these technologies work inside the vehicle. It all felt a little ad hoc and unsettled. Cars are, of course, also full of lots of other things – food, music, umbrellas, washing, toys, feminine hygiene products, other people's stuff, water, spare clothes and the list goes on and on."

08

Art and music event flyer by Broken Fingaz from Haifa.

With any fireside chat, what you need is heat. So what is it that makes a campaign hot? What makes something go viral? How do you create a phenomenon? This is Viagra for any brand, and is the key ingredient for youth communication. A piece of communication is brilliant when a good idea meets craft, with a bit of the right place right time thrown in the mix, and is presented in the correct manner. This is when you get some friction; next thing word is spreading like wildfire. It can be on or off or through or below or above the line. Not that these things really exist any more, or matter.

The ability to see into the world of youth is vital. Then, once you have something going, being able to create a sustainable relationship is your next vital step. One of the key ingredients for this (which then leads on to creating heat) is honesty. This is such an important element that it should be number one in the Ten Commandments (see The Back Section). A great example of honesty creating relationships – which ultimately lead to sales – is the Hans Brinker campaign created by KesselsKramer (see page 41).

It's a strange double world for young people, both physically and psychologically. In the physical world, teens can be treated pretty badly. Many have poor or little education, unless, that is, they are one of the privileged few – but then they might grow up with no street smarts. Most teens leave

↓ **Lee Clow. Global Director Media Arts, TBWA\Worldwide**
↓ **Cliff Lewis. Executive Producer, Droga5**

"Creativity is a means and an end."

"There is an absurd amount of noise, but there are also some genuinely interesting notes in there. Of course, it's still about an 'idea', only now there are more ways to tell the story. We can tell that story online, on film, on paper, on the sidewalk, on your mobile, in store, projected, in a game, on a T-shirt or at the bottom of your coffee cup, but it had better be great. If it isn't, it's trash, instantly. People enjoy good technology and they engage with great, credible ideas. Our role now is to unlock that potential and create the irresistible force, a movement."

school with not enough qualifications and not enough opportunities to succeed, or to realize their true potential, which in turn can lead to crime, deprivation and no creativity in their lives. But in the psychological, hyper-real world of advertising, these street-smart youths are the kings, they are the cool rulers, and this world is theirs for the taking. This is so important to remember. You have to empower youth in both worlds, and in return for this power some heat may be generated for your brand. But what is it really like in this other world? Over to one of the world's most talented youths...

"I try to train my brain to ignore advertising as much as possible. I don't have money most of the time, so I mostly just buy things that I really need, like food and weed. I love the artistic aspect of advertising, even though it's rare that I see something I really like. I hate Facebook and the way it affected real life, also the fact that it feels like everything is so accessible but nothing really excites anyone…"

Broken Fingaz get up on the walls of Haifa.

09

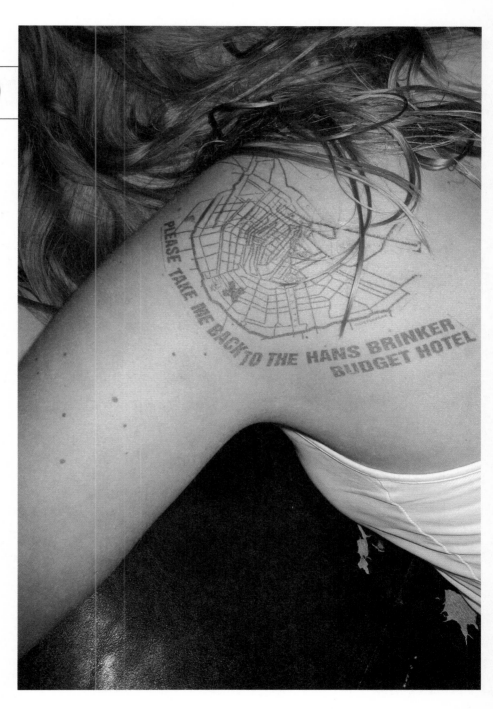

Hans Brinker is a budget hotel/hostel in the heart of Amsterdam. It has been the subject of some great inventive advertising, which has proved very successful in spreading word of how bad the hotel actually is. I spent some time with creative director Erik Kessels, who developed the adverts from the beginning at his agency, KesselsKramer.

What was the hotel like when they first approached KK?

"To be honest, the Brinker has actually improved over the years. Today's Brinker is pretty much OK: it's cleaner than its competitors, with decent facilities. It's still like paying to be in a prison, but a relatively progressive prison. And that's always been part of our strategy: to make the hotel appear a lot worse than it is, which makes it more difficult for people to complain. After all, if a poster promises the worst hotel in the entire world, you can't really say you were misled when there's no toilet roll. At the beginning, the Brinker was pretty intense. Before the security doors, guests were robbed on a fairly regular basis, sometimes with guns. At one point, the Brinker bar was a hang-out for dealers on the hard drugs scene, and there are stories of orgies that spanned entire floors. Most of the time, however, it was a little less extreme in its seediness: basically, it was just a shit hotel."

What was the inspiration behind the campaign?

"The fact that it was a shit hotel. When we first saw the Brinker, all the standard advertising approaches we might have had died. There were no benefits to the consumer, no unique selling propositions, no points of difference. It was just crap. So we decided: why not tell the truth? Why not be brutally honest? It was an approach that worked because it led to a grim kind of humour, a style you don't often see in advertising (even now), and an irony that appealed to the jaded backpackers who might choose the Brinker."

Unique Design

Why do you think it's such a successful piece of advertising?

"Honesty. A willingness to look at yourself, acknowledge your flaws, and say, 'This is me. Fuck off if you don't like it.' There's something about the Brinker's approach that reminds me a bit of good comedians. It's the brand version of the guy who gets up on stage night after night, drinks too much, smokes too much and tells the truth. All the usual impulse control is off, and that leads to a humour people can respond to, even admire, because he's saying the stuff most of us only think. It also leads to a very genuine sort of confidence. Most brands, like most people, go through life carefully tailoring their responses to what they think others will like. The Brinker has the integrity to be itself. If you put aside any individual piece of Brinker communication, it's this long-term attitude that makes the Brinker successful."

10

How do you stay up, ahead, and relevant in the game? This has to be one of the questions most frequently asked in youth advertising. (The other question is, "Where did that great idea come from?" But we all know that this will never be answered!) It is vital to be able to understand what is going on in the world inhabited by the youth, but at the same time you have to be impartial. Let's face it: most of the time we are all way too old to play an active part in this world, but there is still a connection that can be made and sustained, and this is what you need. I'm lucky – I have two teenage kids who pull me up and set me straight in the blink of an eye about what is actually happening in their world. This is what matters.

My advice for anyone who wants to get on in this area is to go out as much as you can. If you can't do that, you're at a real disadvantage! This is one thing I've never been so sure about. You have to be there in body as well as mind to see what's going on – it's not enough just to trawl the Internet. If you're one of the world's top creative directors, then maybe it's slightly different, but you still have to go and talk to people. And I mean really talk to them, not scan a few forwarded emails looking for buzzwords. If I have still got a bit of a clue in my mid-forties, it's because I've been travelling the world taking photos and talking to people for the last twenty years, and I don't stay off the street for long. The most successful people I know in advertising all religiously devote time to

"You stay fresh in the game by being a part of the cultures in which your brand lives. You can't be punk rock from behind a desk. You can't get Aloha in a conference room. And you certainly can't get what is happening in the streets from the 45th floor."

"Advertisers want to communicate with the youth but do not understand them. They do everything in the schematic way that builds upon research into young people's behaviour, but to understand them you have to be one of them, live and dream like them. Therefore, to stay connected, I would hire young creative people who are connected with this multifaceted reality and engage them as spokespersons. If there is something that can change behaviour in society in a considerable way, there is also a possibility of changing the way people perceive the world and its complexity. There is nothing like what the Internet provides in terms of information, entertainment, connection

schlepping along and seeing what it's like down there. Some even employ teams of youths to help them out at this, which often turns into an industry in its own right. I have to touch the ground myself to even come close to getting my head around what's changed in the last five minutes.

Surrounding yourself with fresh young talent may appear to be the obvious answer – but in youth advertising nothing is what it seems at first glance. It's also about state of mind. "New York State of Mind" was originally a Billy Joel song that was borrowed by legendary rapper Nas eighteen years later in his classic song "N. Y. State of Mind". This says a lot about how things work and how things go down in the world of the youth: one

eye on the past and the other on the future, with very little time for the present, unless something out of the ordinary is happening. Talking of a New York state of mind, here's George Lois on the subject of staying up...

and knowledge. Everything today has a dimension much larger than before, because any action is no longer particularly local but a matter of global concern. The youth know exactly how that works and they are at the forefront of this process."

"How do you stay fresh? Easy. I work on stuff all the time. I've got twelve things I'm working on right now that I'm excited about. I only sleep three hours a night in two shifts of an hour and a half. When I get up at 2.30 a.m. I'm really sharp. I've done it all my life. I'm turned on by doing the kind of work I want to do – I'd die without it. In the year 2000 I supposedly retired – my wife said I wasn't retired, I was just tired!

It's terrific to be able to have a mentor in your head. I was lucky, as Paul Rand was mine. I grew up with him in there. I was 14 and he was 26. He was teaching advertising – a young guy writing his own copy and doing his own ads, he

was cantankerous and didn't take any shit from anyone. I saw this and said, you know what – that's what I want to do. That's the kind of guy I want to be. It wasn't the work, as his work was very design-y, whereas mine is: I get an idea, I put it down and that's the job. You want Andy Warhol drowning in a can of soup or Muhammad Ali as Saint Sebastian – that's it, baby! That's the design. He inspired me. He had a book called *Thoughts on Design*, which I still have a copy of, and it's ripped to shreds. Everybody who is successful in this world has people who have helped them. If I hadn't been sent to the High School of Music and Art by my teacher, Miss Angle, I probably woulda wound up being a fucking thug, as I was a rough kid in my neighbourhood. She put me on the subway with a portfolio of my work that she'd collected, and I took a test and got in. It was like the Bauhaus of New York in 1945. She saved my life. I mentor a lot of people and it feels good. I get a lot of emails and try to give them advice.

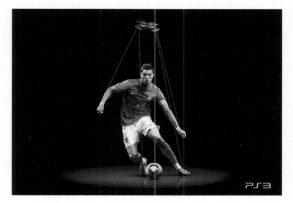

PlayStation 3 ad from BBDO Moscow.

PS3

The best advice I can give is to read my books. You don't have to buy them, go to a library or my website. When you talk to kids they go wild, and I don't talk bullshit. I cut loose. What kids like besides the work is my attitude – I don't take no shit and I tell them not to take any shit. You don't need my personality to do it, all you need is some passion and some heart…and some talent. Everything you work on, you gotta come up with something that is original and shocking. It's my credo: make it a big idea."

11

One agency that has always stayed up is Droga5, and for the launch of Jay-Z's book Decoded, they decided to do something different. I should coco. This is a glorious example of analogue meeting digital and creating something that entertains, yet educates. Executive producer Cliff Lewis took me on a tour of the campaign.

"We launched Jay-Z's *Decoded* in a way that was a first for a published book. We took the book and we 'exploded' it. Page by page. Each page became an event, something in the real world: a Cadillac wrapped on the streets of Brooklyn; the bottom of the swimming pool at the Delano Hotel in Miami; the cloth on a pool table; a rooftop in New Orleans; album covers in a record-store window; huge poster bills in Times Square; a projection inside the Apollo theatre. There were over 200 pieces in all. The pages weren't randomly placed; all 350 were put in locations relevant to the content of each individual page. Fans around the world could actually walk Jay-Z's path, experiencing his story right where it happened.

We built a *Decoded* website, and created digital and analogue infrastructures to release each clue and capture the 'events' as they unfolded in the real world over the thirty-day launch. We tried

The perfect balance between digital and analogue.

to stay as close as we could to the actual book, in terms of the event geography. We were in thirteen cities. It was an incredible amount of work, and I'm privileged to have worked on it; it was a brilliant idea. What was wonderful was the digital and analogue symbiosis, and that the idea was dependent on both.

Each media placement drove fans directly to a digital gaming experience, built on Bing Search and Maps, that allowed them to discover more pages. Over the course of the month-long campaign, fans assembled the book digitally at bing.com/jay-z before it hit the stores. Absolutely every piece was integrated, seamlessly creating a story told over search technology, online maps, social media, bus shelters, billboards, pools, Cadillacs, Gucci jackets. Every component was woven together in service of the greater goal: to allow Jay-Z's fans to experience his story."

12

We all have experienced this moment: you spot something (a pair of sneakers or skate shoes; a pair of jeans; a stainless-steel BMX; a Fibreflex skateboard with lime-green Kryptonics and ACS 651 trucks), the world stands still, and you think, "Fuck me! I gotta have some of that." In this moment you make a personal and cultural connection to a brand, which can stay with you throughout your life, becoming part of your cultural heritage, your DNA. If you can recreate this moment, you can achieve an authentic and lasting connection with the youth, and you are well on the way to having a customer for life. It has taken some time for brands (and the advertising industry as a whole) to realize that these cultural equations are vitally important in consumers'

lives. Remember this when planning and creating any kind of advertising. Brands can make a cultural contribution; it is not always the culture that affects the brand.

My first "fuck me!" moment was with preppy French tennis brand Lacoste. Growing up in a suburb of Greater London in the 1980s was truly boring until I became a Casual. I can remember being on a lads' holiday in Majorca when a friend lent me his Lacoste shirt to go out in. This was an important moment for me; it was almost like I was pulling on a team shirt. I was signing up not just for Lacoste, but also for the Casual movement, and I still feel the same way to this day when I pull on something with a croc over my heart. It's weird

"For me it was *The Six Million Dollar Man*."

"In 1981, it was being sold a £55 Sergio Tacchini T-shirt, travelling to watch the football and then getting into Northern Soul, and then hip hop, largely off the back of that brand. And the reason I work with brands now is because of the Casual movement and the importance of brands to young people who didn't have much money."

LES CROCODILES SONT BELLES.

LA CHEMISE LACOSTE

24/24:BERLIN

LACOSTE L!VE

UNCONVENTIONAL CHIC

24/24:BERLIN on www.lacostelive.com

From French sporting chic to street: the Lacoste journey.

and unexplainable, but I guess that's the stuff you can't bottle; that's the brand seeping into your very soul. And when you look at the cultural history of this moment – how my life was affected by a sporting brand created by a French tennis legend, which I only got into because of its adoption by an English subculture – the DNA becomes pleasantly complicated.

As fate would have it, when I was launching my book <u>Street Knowledge</u> in the US I became involved with Lacoste, who asked me to create a street-art-style advert slap bang in the middle of the Meatpacking District of New York. There was – as always – a marketing agency in between the client

and me. Initially they wanted a design for a vinyl print that would be pasted to the wall like a building or vehicle wrap. Then the agency got back to me to ask, couldn't I paint a design? I guess they got the printed vinyl priced up and saw how much it would cost. Thinking about what I could paint (I only had a day and a half to execute the piece) I had the idea of reversing a giant Lacoste croc out of what appeared to be a fucked-up street art and graffitied wall of fame. I'd go mad on the wall with paste-ups, Krink and Montana paint, lay a giant croc over it and then paint the rest out, leaving some mental drips. I had a seven-foot croc printed from the illustrator of the logo. The big idea was that that the local artists would, I hoped, tag, bomb, stencil and

---

12

55   **That "fuck me!" moment**   ↓ **Scott Nowell. Executive Creative Director, The Monkeys**
↓ **Paco Underhill**

"When I was ten I was given a second-hand pair of Quiksilver board shorts. They were more comfortable than the nylon shorts I'd started my surfing career in, but more importantly they made me feel like I belonged. Not many people had Quikkies in those days, but real surfers did, so despite the fact that I was riding a board I'd found in a council garbage collection, the shorts made me feel like a surfer. The company's grown a little since then, but by and large they've stayed true to their core beliefs and I still buy their shorts today."

"First is my Tempur-Pedic mattress, which gave me much better sleep, and I'm not sure if it was the brand or the product. The second is that the iPod made me a healthier man. It helps me work out and enjoy being active, and the idea of putting music in my ears that isn't jostled when I move is a quantum leap beyond vinyl blasting out of speakers, or my Sony Walkman. When they first released that bright-yellow Walkman I certainly

sticker the wall for the two months it would be up. In the last few weeks I would come by and re-paint the black outline and so the croc would be back, but this time the art would be completely different, and created by the public, not me. This kind of interaction is something that I see as one element of the future of communications.

If you were cynical, you could perhaps dismiss this story as just a brand exercise. You could accuse Lacoste of trying to manufacture a "fuck me!" moment. But it worked because I believed in what I was doing; there was a true connection between the act of creating the advert and my cultural DNA. I wasn't just doing it for the money (which I never got my grubby hands on anyway); I was doing

it because I understood both the brand and the execution (street art in NY). This is paramount for any "fuck me!" moment.

acquired one, but it still needed a belt to carry it, and it was still clumsy to load music onto; it was a sound reproduction device. Moving to the iPod was a complete miracle."

"I grew up in a country where the brands came from three distinctly different cultural traditions – the United Kingdom, the United States and stuff that was homegrown in Australia. It was always fascinating to see how all these different messages, images and products found room in our lives and our homes. Some of those brands and their messages made their way into our language – as they did everywhere, I suppose – and they still slip out today, years later, much to the confusion of my American colleagues."

13

Levi's jacket modelled
by original wearer.
Model : Alonzo, 80, cowboy, Colorado.
Item : Type II jacket.
Stylist : Simon Foxton.
Photographer : Nick Knight.

No brand sums up youth as well as Levi's. From the moment Nick Kamen walked onto that laundromat set, things have never been the same for this most iconic brand of jeans. Brands used to create aspirational worlds that consumers wanted to buy into. Levi's probably offers the best European example from the 1980s: a re-released track, some slick images of a pretty girl and hunky guy, all set in a slightly heightened reality – this would make people pay a little bit more money for the product. It worked for Levi's, establishing them as the best-selling premium-priced jeans. The initial 501s advertising was so successful that the agency (BBH) had to pull the campaign as shops couldn't keep up with demand.

Over the years, the main things that have been consistent throughout Levi's campaigns are humour and spirit. This is what makes the later ads work, even when they feature older people – the spirit of youth is visible, and that isn't restricted to the young. This is something Oliviero Toscani will talk about later on.

"My 'fuck me!' moment was Levi's. I was fortunate to work on an incredible era of advertising for the brand. The learning curve was practically vertical. And I also remember the first time my friend Tony came to school wearing a pair of 501s with button fly. It blew me away: it was a moment in time that was just brilliant. And it was all about the product. It was the same when I heard 'Pretty Vacant' and 'The Place I Love' for the first time. They changed me; I was never going to be the same person. These kinds of moment embed themselves in your DNA and you become the movement. I have never worn another brand of denim."

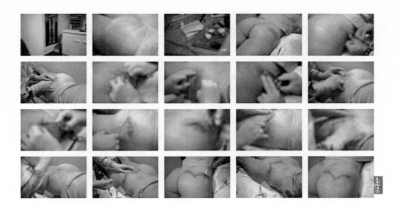

13   ⁵⁹   **Levi's –
Denim dreams**

↓   **Jonathan Kneebone.
Co-founder, The Glue Society**
↓   **Sir John Hegarty. Ad guru**

"We were asked to create a piece of art that stated what we believed Levi's were all about. We felt at heart that jeans equalled youthful rebellion and being bold enough to break convention. The act of stitching someone's bottom felt very Levi's. Some of that rebellion had gone from the brand. We wanted to restore the edge that we felt the brand owned. And the impact it has on a lot of people is one of shock, which feels very appropriate to us."

"The essence of the idea was that Levi's 501s were at the very heart of youth culture. The idiosyncrasies of the product's button fly and the look and the feel of the stone-washed denim were the soul of what made them cool. In other words, you don't hide your differences, but shout about them. Be proud of them."

14

Another brand that has created a lot of "fuck me!" moments around the globe is Vans. Whatever they are doing has worked – I'm a dedicated wearer, and for years I never wore much else other than half-cabs after someone gave me a pair from Thailand at the beginning of the 1990s. I was struck by the timeless design. At that moment the skate look was everywhere, and they stood out as iconic and just simple. This was my second most influential "fuck me!" moment. It has stayed with me to this day: I'm writing this while wearing a pair of Vans and a pair of Levi's at the same time.

A million skaters (and those who don't skate) have had a Vans "fuck me!" moment. There really is no other skate-shoe brand out there that is so authentic and has such a strong link to the culture. It's amazing how Vans have become synonymous with skating. I dropped in on Doug Palladini, vice-president of global marketing for Vans, and asked him what's up.

Why do I still care about Vans when I haven't skated daily for years? (The only shoes I wear are half-cabs.)

"Vans have an uncanny knack of reminding people of something good that happened in their lives. When you put on a pair of Vans, you remember the first time you skated over the light in the deep end of the pool. You remember the first rock show you went to without your parents. You remember your first kiss (and more). No matter where I go on this planet, once people know what I do for a living, a Vans life story cannot be far behind."

What do you think separates the youth from their money?

"Authenticity. Originality. Thankfully, these are two things that Vans has in spades. And also, thankfully, these are two things you can't access just because you possess a bigger chequebook."

FAMILY.

Show, don't tell: Vans' core values proudly displayed.

Is there a single philosophy that runs through each and every Vans advert?

"Sincerity. It's consistently refreshing to market and promote a brand for which bullshit is not required."

Classic vintage: "The World's First Skateboard Shoes".

A book about Vans' work.

15

As the target demographic grows more savvy, the content, concepts and creation of advertising communications have become increasingly akin to entertainment. In some cases they have become entertainment. By now a lot of youth advertising is all but indistinguishable from other forms of non-advertising content, such as documentaries, films, festivals, events and zines (off- and online, mainstream and underground). This is great for the consumer, as well as being great for the creatives and artists working behind the scenes, as they get paid to make high-quality work. The days of the grey corporate-led ads shamelessly trying to sell to the youth are long gone. I spent some time in the US at the end of the 1990s working on advertising for brands that could have been great, if only the agency hadn't been so client-led and afraid to take any risks. It was very difficult to get good ideas through. Now there is a different scenario: the brands are looking at what their audience is into and then following their leads, and this can only lead to great work. These days, I think creative directors are like ringmasters (I've been referred to as a "street middleman"), mediating between cultures, communities and brands. This is when the line between commercial and content becomes blurred to the point where it almost disappears, and things become very interesting.

Today's youth content rolls out in a diverse array of forms. For instance, making use of the different

"Take Red Bull. Although it's not positioned solely as a youth brand, it undoubtedly engages a younger demographic through exhilarating and inspiring event experiences; it literally becomes what you're interested in. It creates situations that are engaging and exciting, and creates fans through its very being. It does not look simply to interrupt; instead it makes content that draws interest the world over. The manner in which it brings experiences to a wider audience is compelling. From disseminating key content to growing talent from the ground up and offering support – these are strong reasons to engage with the brand."

styles of youth fashion and subcultures is now a valid part of selling. The area covered by the term "advertising" has increased to cover so much more than a brand, an agency and the public. In writing this book I wanted to show just how many different elements are vitally important in the creation of effective youth advertising communications. And I can safely say that content is now king.

In 2008, Mother came up with the idea of a feature film, Somers Town, which was funded entirely by Eurostar and directed by Shane Meadows, and went on to win a number of prizes at film festivals. The film was shot around the London terminal for the Eurostar as the building was nearing completion. It is a great project. You can watch the film and there is no overt Eurostar branding or relentless product placement. Now, we are almost at a point where agencies and brands are becoming TV channels, magazine publishers and event producers – and in some cases they already have. In the last few years the majority of the work I've been involved in producing for brands has been more and more about content and less and less about straight advertising. This is an insight into how it will be in the future: advertising becomes entertainment, education and information.

"Brands are no longer just about performance and trust, though those remain fundamentally important; the future is going to be one where they look increasingly at how the two worlds of entertainment and fashion are merging. Brands need to become part of these worlds – where fashion sits alongside the need to be entertained."

Stills from Somers Town.
Classic in b/w.

16

Caroline Pay's quote below sums up the New Look campaign that went out on the UK's Channel 4 as <u>Style the Nation</u> – a star-maker show for aspiring fashion stylists who competed for the chance to win a job. This in itself is mental. Win a job! It says something of the state of the industry, and how talent is regarded. The important thing about this extended campaign (that's essentially what it was) is not only that it was advertising as content, but also that it made brilliant use of available (and free) communications technology – Twitter, Facebook and its own style app. No need for any moody premium-rate phone lines! Using Twitter to vote on who went through to the final was a great live feature and extended the role of the viewer to active participant. Transmedia in full effect.

"The initial brief was to come up with a big idea that had a TV format at the heart of it – a very rare request to come from a client, especially a high-street retailer who didn't just want run-of-the-mill press ads. As an agency we leapt on it, as it was an amazing opportunity to do things differently. The whole campaign started with the expression 'Real-Time Fashion', which summed up the non-stop lives of our audience: girls who are changing their look on a daily basis. If we cast a style barometer over the whole of the UK, this was one of the few high-street brands that could handle it – they can keep up – as they change around 10 per cent of their stock every week. When we came up with the idea of the show it had to represent regional style and how New Look caters to all sorts of different tastes up and down the country.

Host Nick Grimshaw introduces the judges.

The most exciting thing about the show was that it worked in real time – you could play along live online. Someone sitting on their sofa watching at home could have an influence on the programme on screen. One segment was a brief for an outfit, which the viewer then styled online, and by the end of the show a real live model would walk down the catwalk wearing their winning outfit!"

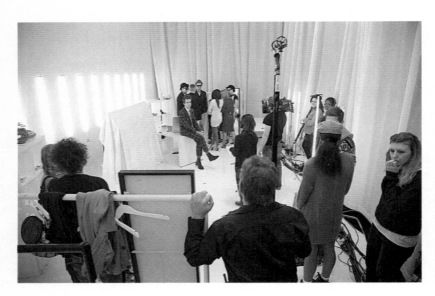

The kids style like they've never styled before.

17

Not so much content, but a physical, useful space, Project FOX consisted of three parts: HOTEL. CONTEST. CAR. Its aim was to nurture and promote young talent. Twenty-one international artists from the fields of graphic design, urban art and illustration were asked to transform a dour three-star hotel in central Copenhagen into a vibrant, cheap and creative lifestyle hotel: the Hotel FOX. The project was a collaboration between Volkswagen and hotel owners Brøchner Hotels as part of the European launch of the VW Fox. The Fox was targeted at the young urban generation, and was designed to be their first car.

What I like about this project is the fact that the hotel lives on long after the actual event and campaign were over. It was handed back to the owners and will go on to cater to a whole new market in young urban tourism. The hotel rooms are not only amazing to stay in but are also cheap and affordable – essential to the young traveller. It's all about youth, urban spirit and mobility. It's about emerging talent and new spaces. Content does matter.

"Why the connection? Project FOX promoted young talent and created new spaces. What counts are the ingredients, the idea, the content and the inner values. Quality. Ideas are the essence of quality. The small car's completely new feeling of spaciousness was one of its many links to the Hotel FOX. From the outside, what used to be known as the Park Hotel looks rather conventional. But inside a breathtaking landscape unfolds, a unique patchwork of the world's most diverse urban life designs. We invited the artists to redesign a total of sixty rooms. Furniture, carpets, wallpaper – they were given free rein to do whatever they wanted. The artists on the project have designed hotel rooms of unique beauty.

Interior/exterior – it's all good!

The VW Fox and Project FOX are designed for a young, urban target group. Keywords: quick trips, city tourism, mobility, wellness escapades, Stockholm, Milan, Copenhagen, targeted enjoyment. Keywords: independence, youth, lifestyle, authenticity, pragmatism, flash events, new heroes, patchwork careers, home cooking, reality checks. The Hotel FOX is a patchwork of different styles, which reflects the lives of young urban professionals. Hugo Boss is combined with H&M, sushi goes with spinach, a Copenhagen hotel meets street art. Chaos? Maybe. But clear criteria are discernible in the merry mix. It's all about the deal! *Carpe diem* meets 'What's in it for me?'"

Hurry up, we're dreaming…

18

Stills from The Glue Society's amazing films <u>V Raw</u> (top) and <u>Metal on Metal</u> (bottom).

The moving image is almost everything. OK, so you've got your big idea, the client is excited and there is a decent budget (this always helps, but is not necessarily the most vital ingredient) – all you need now is to create the imagery, the content. You can have all the things I've just mentioned, but if your choice of moving image is not right then the youth will check out at the very first point of contact. The first impression cliché comes into play here, every time. This makes it tough to create TV spots or position films for the youth market. Once the images are scanned by the audience and are accepted as real, then they may read, watch or engage some more and your relationship with them could develop into something more meaningful.

With the moving image (the still photographic image is covered later on) there is a thin line between the staged and the natural. Documentary-style footage often works best as it can almost appear to be a slice of life: authentic. The flip side of this is the hyper-reality that is often used in adverts for video games, music-related projects and the higher end of fashion (also covered later), which is also effective – as well as entertaining – but way more expensive and more difficult to produce. The stills opposite are from films by The Glue Society that are both moving and challenging; this is vital for creating digital content, as the viewers are kept on the edge of their seats, as well as becoming emotionally involved in what they are seeing.

"My experience is that the more normal you are, the better. Youth is the same as you or me, only sharper."

"Every brief has a duality, so to find out what you really need to be saying, no matter what the brief, you have to understand two things: the business problem and the audience need. Briefs can often be symptomatic. They describe the symptom of the problem but not the actual business problem. That's why we question, to get under the surface to the real issues. Then there's the audience – what are they looking for and how can we make their lives better? By bringing these two aspects of the brief together, you stand a far greater chance of creating something special. You have to believe in what you're doing; if you're not making the world better, why bother? I think you need to make a positive contribution to society. Brands have the power to improve people's lives."

19

Intel's The Creators Project
inspires someone to do just
that – create!

Web 2.0 coupled with increased broadband speeds have made it possible for the masses to watch longer, full-screen, high-quality films online; these are mainly documentaries which, as we have established, are a vital tool for progressive-thinking brands. These films ultimately destroyed the line between online content and advertising. One of the first companies to spot this happening was VICE, the free magazine with a troublemaker attitude and huge devoted following around the world. In 2007, Shane Smith, Suroosh Alvi and Spike Jonze created VBS.tv – an anarchic online TV station with the tagline "Rescuing you from television's deathlike grip", which it did through its docs about youth and street culture. The content was

available on demand and enabled for sharing and embedding, and since people still liked to read, each show also had its own accompanying homepage, updated with exclusive articles and interviews. This is the way forward – each element complements the other, and out of this a unique user experience is created.

In 2006, VICE had set up Virtue, an advertising agency that would take the development of content for brands to another level. Their ambition was to be what MTV was in the 1990s, creating original content that inspires trends and influences the youth market. One of their notable documentary series (sponsored by Palladium shoes) was about cities, covering Detroit and

19   75   **VICE** / Virtue

↓ **Bono. Global ambassador**
↓ **Andrew Creighton. Global President, VICE**

"VBS is punk rock for the 21st century. They are better looking and more rock and roll than we will ever be."

"We cover what we care about, and that's a mix of heavy domestic and international news, underground cultural coverage and our favourite music. The VBS contributor could be anyone from an educated person who gets paid to be a journalist to a random joker off the street who is either smart, funny or crazy."

Blowing up the content with Marshall Headphones.

Tokyo, and topics such as London pirate radio stations, the ruins of New York, and the oil of LA. The agency's website has almost become its own TV station using youth-related celebrities such as Johnny Knoxville (Detroit) and Pharrell Williams (Tokyo).

"There is a funding gap for original content, which can be meaningfully filled by brands. In fact, young people often want and expect more from brands when it comes to entertainment. That said, the key is to make genuinely great, engaging content and not to make long-form advertising. So, while advertisers have provided an opportunity for *VICE* to make documentaries, we've been very conscious that our output needs to be as good or better than non-advertising-funded content.

When referring to the 'viral', I don't necessarily think about specific bits of content. Viral distribution is a product of advancements in digital technology and the proliferation of services that improve communication and peer-to-peer sharing. The phenomenon of viral content simply reflects the nature of how we are able to communicate, and how sharing information from individual to individual is now the norm.

Palladium and Pharrell take Tokyo.

Virals work when great content is fed into these systems. In all of the branded work that *VICE* does, we always try to tell unique and engaging stories. We believe that if we can entertain our audience first and foremost, and provide amazing and memorable experiences, then we have done our job. When conceiving all of these projects, it's a matter of identifying the great stories in that specific field of interest (technology and arts in the case of Intel, or urban exploration in the case of Palladium), and then trying to be as editorially focused as possible in order to represent the story as best we can."

Intel getting behind The Creators Project.

20 [78]

Fly poster from Brick Lane,
London.

How does one convert a viral hit into sales? And, more importantly, how do we know it's working? Between the entertaining ad and the actual sale lies a vast void, which a lot of people don't want to dive into by discussing it directly.

Perhaps attempting to measure the effectiveness of youth advertising is an impossible task – defining the indefinable. How do you capture a group so large and fluid that it never stays still? And the target audience is only half the story. What they're into, what they're watching, reading, wearing – the list is as endless as it is changeable. But this is the key to measuring the effectiveness of advertising in its many guises: understanding how it is influencing the youth.

I think that to find out what works you need to dig deep and dig digital. Now that the old rules no longer apply, it must be difficult to keep up if you are a "traditional" marketer. Digital is hard enough for people to get their heads around, without the added pressure of having to stay up with all the latest trends. By the time some marketers catch on to one thing, the youth have moved on to the next, or even the second or third thing down the line. If we look at the use of phones as a marketing tool, we'll see how they evolve every week through new features and different platforms. It's a bit like learning street knowledge; you have to understand how you can navigate through all the various networks and platforms.

---

20 79   The art of separating the   ↓ David Bernstein. Author
             youth from their money   ↓ Dylan Williams
                                           ↓ Erik Kessels

"Product + Personality = Brand."

"If brands thought of themselves as people who wanted to have a relationship with other people, that would reveal quite a lot about how they should behave. If most people acted the way advertisers do, they'd get punched in the mouth. Actually the best way to secure a long-term, ongoing relationship – particularly young people – might be to start by listening rather than talking. Blend in and slowly but surely get noticed for doing something that's interesting or funny or relevant or cool or different."

"What exactly is youth advertising? It used to mean a Levi's ad on TV, the kind of clip you saw, then bought the jeans, and then bought the soundtrack. These days, you can't measure singles sales because nobody buys them. And measuring a brand's effectiveness in terms of how many units it shifts is considered naive."

The effectiveness of youth advertising varies hugely and depends on the product, the brand and the manner in which the youth are engaged. If we create experiences that enable us (agencies, creatives, brands) to become physically involved in what our audience is interested in, this is a much more effective way of making a connection with the youth demographic. Just putting up analogue or digital images to attract their attention will not engage and will only produce advertising of limited effect. It has to lead to something substantial, something happening in the analogue reality that will inspire or contribute to the lives of the audience. Listen to the voice of the youth. They know what they want.

"First, the most important thing is, obviously, if the product is affordable. Secondly if it's worth buying, if it's of good quality, or does it only have a flashy packaging and wrapper. I also see a lot of fake products being sold in the name of world-known products. For example, my sister gave me a set of Staedtler markers on my birthday on 7th June, two days ago I saw the same stuff with a different label name, but the packing and the look was almost the same and it was ten times cheaper than my real Staedtler markers. So I must say that even if it's stationery, or shoes, or clothing, etc., the world-leading brands should make affordable stuff for people, so they won't be provoked to buy exactly the same but fake stuff to satisfy their needs. I personally don't settle for the cheaper or fake products in stationery, but I wouldn't mind buying a used $300 shoe for $10, because I've nowhere else to go. And when it comes to food or beverages, I have literally stopped eating and drinking outside my home.

N23.COM/LOVE

Air Jordan eternally jumping for the ca$h: fly poster for an old Nike campaign.

20 81   **The art of separating**   ↓ **Sanki King**
the youth from their money   ↓ **Erik Kessels**
    ↓ **Victoria Nyberg**

I believe the more popular the world-leading fast-food chains and restaurants are, the more their quality is getting worse. It's like they don't even care about quality any more, they just want their money, even if they have to stuff their stuff in your mouth and snatch the money outta your pockets."

"'Youth' communications today are described in terms of 'movements' and effectiveness is gauged in terms of Facebook fans. Don't get me wrong – it's an exciting new world, particularly for creatives – but I'd imagine that anyone interested in measuring what we do will have a harder time now than ever before. The old line, 'I know half my advertising budget is wasted, but I don't know which half,' is truer in the 2010s than it was sixty years back."

"For me it's all about moving people and changing consumer behaviour, regardless of whether it is directed towards youth or not. To me, a

Keith Haring posthumously designs for Adidas.

successful and effective campaign is when we affect how young consumers think, feel and behave with a brand. Digital is a great platform for achieving this, and as it's becoming an increasingly engaging medium, the effectiveness of advertising in general is increasing."

Elvis shills his new Greatest Hits. Caption by passing youth.

21

Using a smartphone, AKQA took the interaction with your TV and football team to the next level. Interesting stuff indeed for all footy fans who want to get closer to their team. Fans seem to get inklings as to what's about to happen in a match: Star Player enables them not only to test these instincts, but also to compete with friends. This is the key to the idea: it creates a digital experience out of an already existing fan behaviour. This is also why AKQA believed the idea would succeed. It's not a digital idea, it's a football idea, created by football fans. Digital is merely the medium for it.

AKQA's research told them that up to 50 per cent of sports fans watch a game while at the same time texting friends, using Facebook or surfing the Net. Star Player taps into this "dual-screen" behaviour by adding another dimension to the match. Getting fans to predict match moments gives them "skin in the game", allowing them to extend and heighten that feeling of anticipation that makes live football compelling.

"Heineken sponsors the UEFA Champions League and has done since 2004. The business question was clear: 'What is Heineken bringing to the party?' From an audience point of view, people are already watching football and having a good time, so how can the brand contribute? How do you amplify the experience?

All platforms are covered. Score.

The idea for Star Player came up in conversation between several football fans here at AKQA: why not tap into fans' natural competitive banter? At key moments in matches – whether corners, free kicks in dangerous positions, teams attacking fast on the break or winning a penalty – fans don't just sit silently watching to see how the action plays out. They go with their instincts and anticipate – telling everyone that a penalty is about to be missed, a goal scored or a free kick smashed straight into the wall. What we created was the world's first multi-platform live dual-screen football game where fans play along live with their favourite teams, predicting key match moments to earn points and compete with friends."

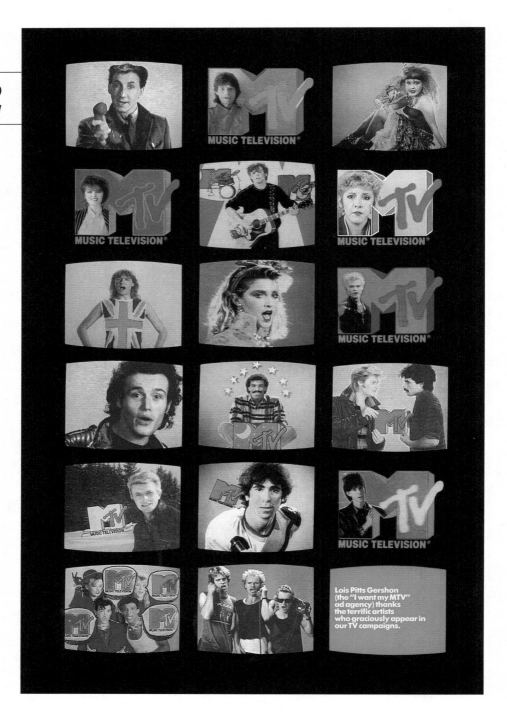

Lois Pitts Gershon (the "I want my MTV" ad agency) thanks the terrific artists who graciously appear in our TV campaigns.

George Lois is a proper bona fide advertising legend. He has worked as an art director since the 1950s, for CBS, DDB and then <u>Esquire</u> magazine (creating more than ninety-two covers). In 1960 he set up Papert, Koenig, Lois, which was the first ever ad agency to go public. He was also solely responsible for the launch of MTV when it was a start-up, and it was his talent that ensured its success. It was an honour for me to sit down with him in his New York apartment one spring morning and have a chat over breakfast. George Lois is the most energetic and enthusiastic 80-year-old I've ever met, which, I think, is one of the secrets to his success.

How do you see the effectiveness of youth advertising?

"For a long time now people advertising to youths have thought that young people hate advertising – as they should – when it asks for a sale. But advertisers go wrong when they seemingly don't ask for a sale. They try to do hip commercials, and you can't remember the brand name – they're total rubbish. I took a class a coupla years ago and the kids described a beer commercial, and they all loved it, but when I asked what brand it was for they couldn't agree. I tell kids that they have to ask for a sale. In advertising you have to stun, and the viewer has to remember something visual and the words, the brand. There should be a mnemonic that is visual and a mnemonic that is verbal. If it doesn't have that, it sucks. You should be able to say the brand name and people immediately have the image in their head. Every product in the world is just as good as the competition. The job of the advertising is to give

Reebok Pump locker room action with a very clean-cut Dennis Rodman, 1989.

the perception that yours is better. You don't just say it's better; you show it with an idea that is so sharp and so memorable that you fall in love with the advertising. Literally. Great advertising makes the coffee taste better. It makes the car drive better. It's not lying. It just becomes part of the product."

How did you get involved with MTV?

"In 1982 they call me up. They're all young – 26, 27 – and I was 50 already, and I wasn't really a rock fan. MTV had been in business a year and didn't have a single cable operator signed, as everybody in the music business thought they were a joke and believed it would destroy their sales. Advertisers didn't think anyone would buy products on a show that talked to kids. I even heard that when MTV made their presentation at a cable convention in Miami, people were snickering and laughing at the guys on the stage – that's how stupid they thought the idea was. Anyway, they want me to do a trade ad for the cable operators. I tell them to forget it – those guys just sit around smoking cigars, thinking that the kids are dumb and getting shitfaced on pot all day. What they needed was a campaign to shove it down their throats. First I changed the logo. I used one with lips in it. I wanted to do a quick-cut commercial using their music videos to establish a feel, and towards the end a voice says, 'If you don't get MTV where you live, pick up the phone, dial your local cable operator and say' – and we cut to a rock star like Mick Jagger, who picks up

Tommy takes on Times Square. And Ralph, Calvin and Perry...

the phone and says – 'I want my MTV!' They
looked at me, looked at each other, then said,
'You know, George, you couldn't get a rock star
in ten million years, they hate us and don't want
any part of it.' I said, 'First of all I'll get a fucking
rock star, and then you run that commercial and
50,000 kids will see it and a hundred will call up
the cable operator and ask for MTV.' They gave
me a week to get a rock star, and then come back
with another idea. I know I walked out and they
all looked at each other and said, 'What the fuck
was that!' as they had been trying to get a rock
star for ever.

I happened to know Bill Graham so called him
and said I'd love to get Jagger just to stick it up
their asses, and he gave me Jagger's number
in London. I told him who I was and he knew
my work and said he would do it. He said he'd
be in NYC on the following Monday, and where
would I like to shoot him? I wasn't prepared,

Kennedy without tears, 1964.

so I gave him the name of a studio I hoped
I could get. Come Monday we wait forty-five
minutes and the door opens and it's Jagger,
everybody in the place breathes a sigh of relief,
and he hugs me and says he's brought a couple
of friends, Pat Benatar and Pete Townshend, and
maybe I wanted to shoot them too. I was so happy
that if he were a girl, I'd have fucked him!

So we shoot and edit a commercial with this
footage and whatever music videos, and we run
it in San Francisco – four spots in the middle of
the night. Bob Pitman gets a call a few hours later
from the cable operator telling him to 'get that
fucking commercial off the air'. Yes, sir… 'And
I'll take it – I'm getting thousands of fucking
calls.' In six months we had 92 per cent of the
cable market. *Time* magazine ran a cover story
saying 'America wants its MTV'. That's the way
it happened."

23

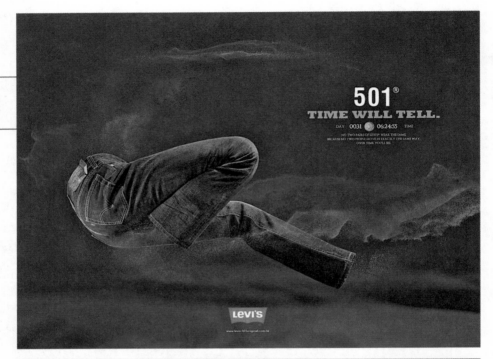

Digital desktop program that ages your Levi's over time.

This is where it begins to get a bit different. The young creatives, strategists and thinkers who have grown up immersed in the digital world understand so much more about what is possible right now. Us older folks can't even begin to compete with these talents, and we shouldn't try to. The way forward is to surround yourself with people who know more about it than you do.

I can remember having the task of trying to sell Woolworths (the South African equivalent of M&S or Bloomingdale's) a website, back in 1998. I'd designed a working offline version, and after demonstrating it to a room full of middle-aged South Africans, one of them turned to me and said, "Very nice – but I don't think Woolworths really needs this!" I had to step up and try to explain how important the Internet was going to be, and why Woolworths should have a presence there. I think what finally convinced them was the fact that their competitors were having a site designed. It's a bit like today when every brand has to have a Twitter or Facebook logo on their ad, because they feel they have to show they're keeping up. This is not the right reason to do it.

People will only connect with your brand online if you are offering something else, something value-added that isn't available in a print, TV or online advert. As I've already mentioned, the digital element is the vital catalyst in

23 93 The digital domain

↓ **Damon Stapleton. Executive Creative Director, Saatchi & Saatchi Sydney**
↓ **Mark Seidenfeld. IT genius**

"The trick for marketers is to learn to maximize the value of the traditional media by incorporating digital. Already many brands try to drive people to their websites, but I'm guessing that, in the not too distant future, all advertising, whether it's TV, print, radio or billboard, will have an interactive component. That's the kind of relationship that digital-savvy consumers are starting to demand. Digital is forcing advertising to throw out the rule book. Advertising is obsessed with labelling things, but what's happening can't be labelled. Even Cannes Lions acknowledged this when it took the word 'advertising' out of its festival name. It's as if advertising is moving out of its frame, out of the art gallery and into the streets."

"The original form of targeting was based on the media channel – a financial paper is likely to be read by upscale people, so I'm not going to sell detergent in the *Wall Street Journal*. The Internet just makes that so much more effective. There the advertising revolution, and although the good idea is still paramount, digital is the indispensable platform from which to launch these ideas. And it is constantly evolving. Someone's probably designed something new just as you've read this paragraph.

The process of selling and getting a product or brand out there steps up a gear when technology is mixed with equations, thanks to developments such as Google AdWords and other information-tracking apps and technologies. Then add this to the one thing that makes people connect digitally – an authentic narrative – and you're cooking. This is when it becomes genuinely powerful. Narrative-driven communications that actually

have something to say about the consumer's life are what makes digital content go viral.

are multiple technologies out there to track user behaviour: from the traditional 'cookie' to the 'pixel counter'. The pixel is an advanced version of the cookie. On a webpage there are a bunch of pictures that you download, and one of these is a one-pixel-by-one-pixel transparent square that you can't see. It runs a script that sends back a bunch of reliable information. This type of business is quite big, and there are various pixel providers, such as Google Analytics. What the publisher or website owner wants is a better understanding of what their visitors want – what they liked, what they read and how long they spent there.

I need to show the advertiser that when they're looking for skateboarders, my system will help target them better than any other system out there. To get a system that really works you have to use several components: the data source acquisition, multiple processing systems and the sales system – which is the actual ad engine.

Rehabstudio's Spots v Stripes game for Cadbury. Addictive as chocolate.

We're not writing a lot of software; we're mainly buying multiple components and putting them together. Almost every e-commerce site sells or shares data about your purchases with marketers. In the US this is still legal and they can share it with your name, address, email, etc. Through various efforts we can make a deal, say, with Amazon, and in a country where I can tap the personal identifying information, Amazon will allow me to place this pixel in their checkout. When you go in there, the system will give me back anonymized information, and I can then match up this unique ID with your other web behaviour, so now I know that not only do you go to this or that site, but also how much you're spending and on what. This may sound scary, but really every store is doing it anyway. This is a practice that has been going on for centuries, from ancient guilds to the Tesco Club Card."

24

The viral video has become a powerful tool. It can travel beneath the radar: with no or little censorship, even the most controversial imagery and ideas can be used to generate some heat and get word of the brand out there. Often it is a campaign within a campaign, or run on the side with little or no connection to what might be happening in the mainstream communication.

"If you've got a good campaign these days, you can go viral in a couple of minutes. With print, radio or TV, it's finished when the campaign goes to print or is aired, but digital works in a different way. It's just the start when you go live – who knows how it will then evolve and change? You have to get so many parts of the puzzle right for it to be effective. One-on-one communication can happen in various ways – it can be through audio or visuals. You can provide so many types of content. It feels much more exciting and there are so many opportunities. It seems like there are no limits, even though there are."

↓ **Juan Vandervoort**
Head of International, PIAS

"Virals are really important these days – after all, social networks are one of the main drivers in building a fan base. But everything comes and goes. For music artists, right now it's more important to have a viral video than a remix. MySpace came and went, then there was Facebook (still hugely important), but when it comes to music YouTube is where it's at for bands. Labels can monetize YouTube videos and get a little money each time someone watches one (apart from in Germany). There are some bands that do videos for each track on their new album, but, as I said, everything comes and goes, and I'm sure we'll reach a point where even fans don't want to sit down and watch all that. Either way, it has been a major shift: it's not about high-budget glossy music videos any more, it's about cool, edgy, very often low-budget virals."

25

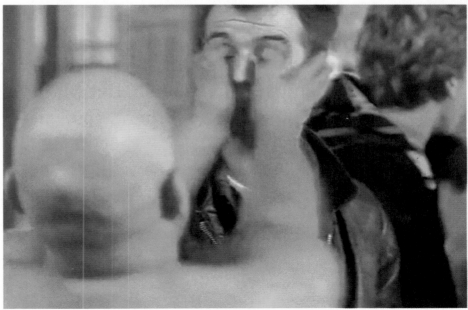

Slightly left field, but still relevant, Steve Henry's "You know when you've been Tango'd" TV spot for the Britvic fizzy orange drink is an example of viral video before it was invented. We all know it: a guy drinks from a can of Tango and a fat bald orange bloke runs up and slaps him on the chops, but is seen only when the footage is played back in slo-mo! Kids talked about it, copied it, and it may well have been influential in the "happy slapping" craze that got the middle classes chattering. People even went out and made their own videos, which are still showing on YouTube today. I think the drink sold pretty well as a result, and we all got to hear the late, great Gil Scott-Heron rapping the immortal tagline: "You know when you've been Tango'd!"

"For Tango, we had a lot of fun playing around and trying stuff out for a while. The result was that a lot of our ads were virals, pre-viral. The Blackcurrant Tango ad only ran six times in paid-for media, but kept cropping up in other media – magazines, TV shows, etc. Orange Tango was similarly something that climbed out of the 'advertising ghetto' and into mainstream culture. It was talked about, copied, played with. Some people even see a link with the later phenomenon of 'happy slapping', although that's not something I'd particularly want to pursue – 'happy slapping' is a really stupid phenomenon. But when you put something interesting out there, you can't control what happens with it."

26

Rather more risky, but a clever example of the viral, is the Diesel "SFW XXX" YouTube phenomenon. This quickly racked up over one hundred million hits with its cheeky nod to what you can and can't watch at work. Branded SFW ("safe for work"), it was a montage of retro porn video clips but with the offending parts (!) painted out and replaced with cartoon images of games, fluffy animals, DJ decks, vegetables, even a potter's wheel! It was created by the Viral Factory and spawned/inspired a piece of renegade advertising from the Cousins directing team in the US – who we will come across later, if you'll pardon the pun.

"Viral videos have not changed advertising in as much as the complete 'world of advertising' has changed since the global popularization of the Internet. Viral videos have simply arisen to fill an opportunity in the new system of advertising: advertising is now social, 2.0, blah blah…and all the other bullshit things marketing people are now saying in the wonderful world of 'everyone saying a lot of nothing'. What has come from this is companies no longer go to agencies and ask for TV ads. Now they go to the agency and ask for a viral video (and it's cheap, too!), and this is the most absurd thing about how companies perceive and work in this new era. One cannot ask another person to do a 'viral' video: you could ask them to do something that has the 'potential' to be viral. Then an organic/complex/quantum system begins spreading. Or not spreading. Also, every time anyone says 'viral video', a bunny rabbit is killed using a gruesome random form of medieval capital punishment."

Porn becomes pinball with Diesel.

"Viral advertising was the first online content-driven expression of earned media – and arguably drove people to recognize it (even though PR has the true claim to being the first earned media). The explosion of online video, of which viral is just one part, has made brands realize there is value in making content that gets shared, beyond fluffy and intangible 'brand value'. When a client is paying 20 cents CPV [cost per view] to distribute a video, and the next guy has made a viral video that is costing .01 cents CPV to distribute because it's being shared, there's an immediate financial incentive to create better content. So suddenly we're seeing viral potential being baked into film content, which is not viral marketing – and that means advertising is getting perceptibly better. But, of course, there's still an awful lot of crap about!"

27

This is a good time to mention augmented reality (AR) and how powerful a tool it is going to be for advertising and brands in the near future. AR, an extension of virtual reality, is a real-time digital addition to something taking place in the physical world. Using smartphones or large video screens, brands can grab the viewer's attention and then entertain or inform using AR. The digital interacts with the real in front of the user's eyes. Forward-thinking Amsterdam-based agency Gummo used AR when they were asked to design a series of stamps for TNT post, the Dutch postal service. Each stamp featured an architectural project, and visitors to the website could then use a webcam to explore a 3D version of the image online.

"As the buildings hadn't been built yet, the designs for the stamps had to be made from the architects' sketches and models. We took our inspiration from the Cubism movement, as Cubist artists also faced the challenge of showing objects from multiple angles on a flat canvas. The visual language used for the design of the stamps refers to this art history. Each of the buildings was portrayed in two stamps: one showing the building itself and a special marker stamp containing the augmented reality code.

We wanted to create a consistent look for all the stamps, so to make the markers complement the portraits, we used abstract shapes derived from the characteristic shapes of each of the buildings. The design of these stamps was crucial for making the augmented reality code work, and making the buildings come to life through the webcam. Therefore we had to incorporate ingredients such as a thick, black border and

Nederland
2011

Studio Marco Vermeulen & HAU
Parkeertoren Nederland

www.toekomstinbeweging.nl

**AR stamps: paving the way for
what will soon be possible.**

conduct multiple tests to ensure that the stamp designs would still work – even after the postal service had stamped them."

"I don't think the Internet has changed the game; it's technology! I can't remember what it was like living without Internet, and the generation younger than me can't even switch between the online and offline worlds."

Nederland
2011

Studio Marco Vermeulen & HAU
Parkeertoren Nederland

www.toekomstinbeweging.nl

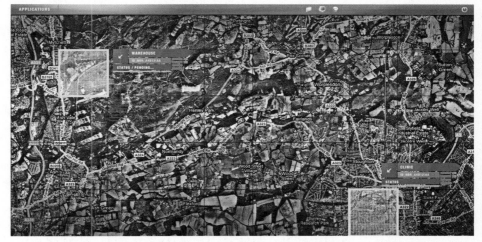

Rehabstudio's original brief was to build awareness and sales of a new "mystery" flavour of the premium Doritos snack. They answered this by creating a digital-integrated brand experience combining long-form narrative storytelling, high-tech online gaming and some clever word-of-mouth marketing with traditional on-pack promotional techniques. iD3 was a breakthrough piece of online brand entertainment designed to push the boundaries of the advergame genre. The three-part, feature-film-length digital adventure was a unique blend of live-action film and 3D gaming, with secret levels for hardcore gamers and integration with Facebook Connect, morphing players' profile photos into video scenes for a truly immersive, personalized consumer experience.

Created for the launch of Doritos' new limited-edition mystery flavour, the game's narrative expanded upon the intrigue. In London's shady underworld, an identity-theft ring has stolen your identity and you have been coerced by the police to go undercover, track them down and expose the criminal mastermind behind the gang. Game players are put in the driving seat, deciding their fate as the hero of this interactive film, by choosing the direction of the plot.

"We find that we're in a kind of sweet spot in between the old-guard ad agencies that don't get the joke, and the younger teams who do. Since we understand the target audience, our digital ideas are a lot more effective than traditional agencies'. There are so many channels to exploit and people to talk to, so there are more opportunities to be creative and do new stuff. When doing a pitch you need to think about how you can be relevant to an audience, as there's nothing worse than an agency trying to be cool – they'll be shut off and will face negativity from their audience because they're faking it. A lot of what we do is a little bit of entertainment, along with a few tools that allow users to remix the work. This lets young people express themselves, which is quite enabling for them."

29

Victoria Nyberg studied at the Berghs School of Communications in Stockholm and now works in London. We met over a boardroom table one night, while brainstorming ideas on how to revive the fortunes of a budget airline. She has a great future ahead of her and represents wholeheartedly the new breed of advertising talent for whom understanding digital is a reflex action. The piece of work that put Victoria on the advertising radar was a 2010 Twitter campaign called "Don't Tell Ashton". The brief was to promote Berghs and its graduating class to the advertising industry and to attract international talent to study at the school, and more specifically on the Interactive Communication programme, which was only a few years old and lives somewhat in the shadow of Hyper Island and Berghs' own art/copy programme. "Don't Tell Ashton" brought it out into the spotlight. Victoria was one of five students who put their heads together and came up with a killer idea that would not only spread word about their course, but also introduce the students to creative directors. Over to Victoria.

Strategy:
"We knew that creative directors have little time and are approached by tons of students each day, so we figured speaking directly to them wasn't the way to go. Instead we created something that could catch anyone's attention, but would spread word about us in the advertising world. The core of the project was to demonstrate our understanding of digital by highlighting the new phenomenon of 'social currency'. We identified Twitter as the perfect place to execute, based on the behaviour tweeters demonstrate: they're sharing information and love/hate for a brand with their fellow peers, each tweet influencing others' perceptions. We just needed to show them how much impact one person's tweet could make, compared to others'."

Execution:

"We invited people to join the world's first artwork made by Twitter users. People 'paid' to get on the artwork with a tweet, and the more followers you reached, the bigger your photo was in the frame. The only person with enough followers to fill the entire piece alone was the most followed person on Twitter at the time, Ashton Kutcher. That's why we urged people to #Don't Tell Ashton."

Someone told him: the team hang with Ashton.

Result:

"The artwork was completed three days after launch, reaching over four million people from 151 countries. The top three participating countries were the US, the UK and Brazil. All major advertising industry press wrote about us, including Mashable, PSFK, etc. We also reached press all around the world. Creativity Top 5 ranked the project number one in May 2010. After handing Ashton the finished artwork, he finally tweeted and wrote about the project on Facebook, reaching his 5 million+ Twitter and Facebook followers. After graduating, the majority of the twenty-two students from the Interactive programme at Berghs got jobs all over the world, and the following year the programme attracted students from fifteen nationalities. Ashton is making a new sitcom inspired by the project called *Don't Tell Steve*. And each time we win an award, the word keeps spreading."

Millions of advertising pounds are now being channelled into what's called social shopping, or s-commerce. With the explosion of Facebook, Twitter and other international social networking sites, a high percentage of the budgets that were previously spent on TV, print or other interactive/digital media are now going straight into the pockets of the companies who run social media. This is what word of mouth has become. Social networking is the grapevine, the water cooler, the local pub where people swap stories and talk about what's hot and what blows. And it's only just started.

You have to adapt your business to sell to people in the way they want. Customers are willing to pay the right price for the right product with the right delivery, but you have to build the right structures from which to do this. What we're seeing is a partial shift back to commerce as we used to know it. Paco Underhill's book <u>Why We Buy</u> looks at how the market used to be a social place where you discussed politics, gossiped about the neighbours, and talked with the people who made the products about how and why they produced them, and then you bought them. We then shifted into a mass-market culture where you drive your hybrid car to the superstore and buy your products at a reduced cost, but you pay in other ways, as the experience is dehumanized and, well, crap. It's generic and cold. Alternatively, you can go online and get

"If we describe social networking as the journey between London and Berlin, we haven't left Heathrow yet. The social networking platforms that we know now are basically castles built on sand, because 21st-century youth is distinctly promiscuous. What is cool today may be very uncool tomorrow. And that is true with Twitter, Facebook, MySpace. At one point we thought that Yahoo was going to run the world!"

"Digital is the best thing that could have happened to advertising. Sorry to put it so abruptly, but in our world of 140 characters, there's no room for verbosity. For decades, advertising has been cruising along, secure in the belief that we control the message and that people want to hear what we have to say. Digital has changed all that. Digital has created a generation of consumers who have a world of knowledge, a wealth of opinions and the means to express them."

the same products even cheaper, and this is something that can't be competed with. But the times are a-changing. There is now a growing demand for a great shopping experience, and this is being provided by local specialist stores, where the owner (who actually works in the shop) knows everything about the products – but the products cost more. Mix this with technological innovations such as Square (payment via your smartphone) and you have a winning approach. Technology has advanced far enough for us to be able to regress back to a more culturally significant encounter when we're shopping. You can wander into a bookstore, chat to the guy about a book and walk out with it. You don't need the hassle of waiting in line and then pulling out your card so they can take an impression of it. It makes it a simpler, more enjoyable experience.

We are rapidly moving away from the old advertising model, which was based around bought media and broadcast push-messaging, and all that kind of stuff. Some people are genuinely underestimating the role that digital media is playing in all of this. It can mean a million different things – commerce or social or mobile or search or all the other things that are possible today because of the thing called digital. This places even more emphasis on the idea that to understand an audience you need to be out in the field getting under the skin of how they behave and why. The opportunities in this wonderful,

30   115   **Social shopping**

↓ **Anne-Fay Townsend. Strategist and Co-editor, BigShinyThing.com**
↓ **Chris Colborn**

"I think the potential of social shopping is massive, particularly if you incorporate collaborative filtering. Just consider, for instance, how much fashion fans or music fans depend on each other's recommendations and opinions. This, married with a mass platform such as Facebook (or whatever replaces it), means that brands could insert themselves just at the pertinent part of the conversation or – better still – initiate it."

"It's been a growth phenomenon, and there are a number of ways to look at it: the integration of social commerce into e-commerce, digital commerce, the rise of social currencies, and the increasing mobilization of social commerce. An example would be Amazon, who have always had a dozen social features on their product description page, but they weren't really integrated into a social site, so it felt like you were shopping in a giant warehouse alone, with all these notes left behind by people who had

digitally connected world are significant; there
is no other reason why companies like Google or
Facebook have stolen tens or hundreds of millions
out of the global marketing spend, all of which
used to go on broadcast, TV and radio, outdoor
and newspaper advertising. The budgets haven't
grown that much; the money is just shifting.

been there before you. But Amazon now has a
relationship with Facebook that will allow you
to log in with Facebook Connect, bring all your
friends with you, and figure out what they have on
their Amazon wish lists. Amazon will scrape their
Facebook pages to see what ideas they can offer
that are relevant and will turn into commerce.
We've seen an increased use of the 'like' button,
and brands such as Levi's use Facebook with their
Friends Store, where you view products liked by
your peers or by aggregate to see what is popular.
There is a massive influx of social integration
expanding commerce within the digital space.

We've also seen the growth of things like
Facebook stores. There is a company called
Gloople that gives small and medium-sized
businesses the opportunity to set up Facebook
and Mobile stores, analyse group purchasing
behaviour, promote via Twitter – so it's a
packaged solution to democratize social media

selling to 'mom and pop' shops. We're seeing this shift from people talking about what they're buying or thinking about buying to being able to make those purchases right there in the social environment. Facebook has become a parallel to the proper web, as people are spending hours in there. The explosion of s-commerce has come about because of things like Facebook credits, and deals with all the major Facebook games companies, who shift a lot of products with the credits. We're now seeing a world where Facebook is one of the ten most populous countries on the planet, so an entire social media currency exists parallel to the physical currency, and it's growing significantly in volume because of the transactions conducted within this world. A lot of the youth may go into a Tesco or Walmart and buy a Facebook credit card and then spend those credits in the virtual world. This becomes very interesting. Then you've got the mobile and location-based services and all these Groupon deals. It is all moving away from the idea of a future purchase, to an immediate deal. This makes it a different world that we're rapidly heading into…"

Social shopping, Rwandan style.

31

CP+B's cheeky online campaign may have got them in trouble with Facebook, but it made us all think about how fickle we are when it comes to our online "friends".

"CP+B did some great campaigns for Burger King, and the 'Whopper Sacrifice' campaign baffled me from the beginning. It really tapped into a truth about the superficial nature of friend relationships on Facebook, and how 'little' a Facebook friend was worth. The deal was: un-friend ten friends, and get a burger. My immediate reaction, of course, was: 'Would I insult my friend to save $3? Probably not.' However, I thought the campaign's premise was hilarious. The funniest thing is that it let the sacrificed friends know they were sacrificed for a burger on their Facebook wall.

The campaign quickly went viral and was adopted by over 20,000 users, who sacrificed 200,000 friends for free Whoppers. Sadly, the application was shut down by Facebook as quickly as it started, citing privacy concerns. Regardless, the application was beautifully constructed and the idea was perfect. Burger King built in the ability to share it, the incentive to use it, and added just enough humour to make the campaign a hit. It may not have brought in a great deal of profit, but Burger King has generated buzz and raised awareness of the 'Whopper Sacrifice' and their brand in general, which will lead to more brand recognition, recall and memorability."

"It is easy to overemphasize the impact of a single campaign or what a stand-alone piece can accomplish, but also to undervalue what a long-term cooperation between client and agency can achieve. However, 'Whopper Sacrifice' actually did have a lasting impact in terms of activating people – as a result, Facebook shut down the functionality after thousands of people had been un-friended. That was pretty remarkable. Personally, I'm a big fan of 'The Great Schlep' by Droga5 from the US presidential election in 2008 for the way it created conversation and activated people in so many ways, bringing benefits on political as well as personal levels. It was so clever, all the way from strategy to execution. People don't talk about advertising; they talk about what interests them, and sometimes that is advertising. This campaign is a good example of great advertising."

Burn those Facebook friends. Get a Whopper.

ANTI-DRUG FACEBOOK TIMELINE FROM ISRAEL

32

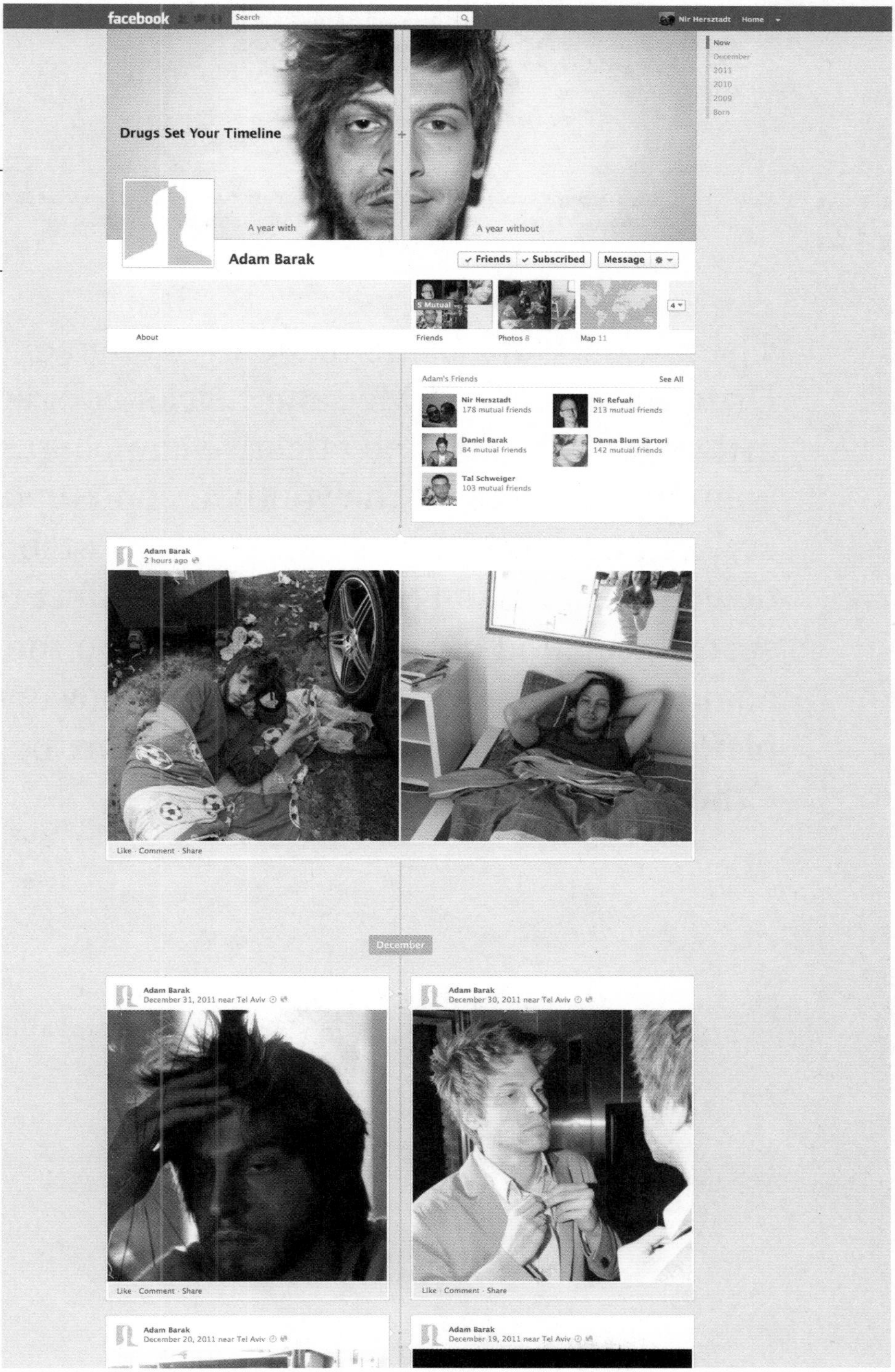

This campaign came in at the eleventh hour. It is a great use of social media to spread a great message: drugs fuck you up. McCann Erickson Israel took the Facebook Timeline and created an almost real-time campaign to show how not to ruin your life. By creating a fictional user – Adam Barak – to alert people against drug use, and then using images of Adam's "life", they divided the Timeline showing Adam under the influence of drugs in one column ("A year with"), and the same Adam during this period without using drugs in the other ("A year without"). In this "split page" Timeline, the viewer can retrace Adam's choices and stages of demise or happiness.

"The mutual work being made by the Israel Anti-Drug Authority and McCann Erickson Israel brings to life smart and effective campaigns communicating with the youth in contemporary style. In our anti-marijuana campaign we boldly decided to abandon the strategic attempts to spread fear, and instead chose to talk to the young audience at eye level and to use an innovative platform, utilizing the most progressive tool – the Timeline."

Drugs Set Your Timeline

A year with   A year without

33

Is selling to young women any different from selling to young men? Yes. It has to be, I guess. It really depends on the product and the brand, but when we look at communications aimed at women, most of the work is produced for fashion or cosmetics. Forget perfume advertising, as this is way out there in a world of its own (often a very strange, pretentious one) and is always seen as a bit of a joke, except by the brand behind it. Ultimately advertising comes down to having a great idea, regardless of which sex you are selling to, and this will shine through if the product is something that is relevant to a youth audience. Narrative is important, but more important is human nature.

There is often a lack of imagination in fashion advertising. The luxury brands are constantly worried about jeopardizing their prestige status, and then there are the usual commercial pressures, which means that every brand is trying to use a similar, tried-and-tested formula to get the highest possible return. This means that everyone ends up using the same photographers, the same models and the same communication channels. For the youth market, some of the more accessible brands – H&M, Primark and Zara – are becoming increasingly innovative through an understanding of social media channels and of just how important (and valuable) user-generated content can be.

"There is some data to suggest that men and women, in the American market at least, respond to different kinds of advertising and brand messages. That data points to the sense that women want a story and men want facts. I think it is more subtle and more complicated than that. Women are frequently making purchases on behalf of larger groups of consumers (their families, kids, in-laws, etc.). Value and price are two very different things and should not be conflated when it comes to understanding purchasing behaviour and thus selling. And it is also influenced by what the object or service is to be used for – is it household, personal? Of course, age, race, class and culture all play a part here, too!"

One thing is certain: regardless of gender, the youth love to spend, thanks to their exuberance, lack of responsibilities and tendency to live for the moment! At the point of purchase, boys are more selective, while for girls it depends more on their desires at that point in time – on the imagery or storyline or certain something that has stayed with them for longer than a nanosecond and ultimately influences what they buy. It also depends heavily on what type of product you're selling. A lot of products are gender-neutral, i.e. our desire for it is not related to our sex. Then there are products that are extremely gender-specific – the classic product categories here are beer and cosmetics. To be successful in selling these, you have to understand the emotional need of the customer and the role of the product in a broader context: beer is very much about male bonding, and cosmetics are about making the best out of the looks you're given.

One industry in which nothing is what it seems is gaming. Worth around $56 billion in 2010, the massive video-game industry was traditionally the realm of the geeky, awkward teenage boy. Not any longer. In 2011, according to the Entertainment Software Association (ESA), some 72 per cent of households in America play video games and 42 per cent of the people playing those games are female. OK, so the average age of the player is 37, but you can see where I'm heading. A high percentage of these female game players have been snared by new-media games such as Angry

"First, let's look at the similarities. The reason why advertising is focused on a younger and younger audience is that young people still have the mistaken belief that product acquisition is transformational – meaning that most of us, after we reach a certain age, realize that when we acquire something it doesn't turn us into somebody we weren't before we acquired it.

If I look at a seven-year-old child in the favelas of Rio de Janeiro, their knowledge of brands might be just as good as a child of the same age who is growing up in St John's Wood in London.

In terms of what is male and female, as we deal with youth, we know that girls often mature earlier and therefore the images that we use for them tend to be somewhat more advanced than for males of the same age. The hormonal changes happen in females sooner, young women tend to be much better at expressing themselves and

Birds on their smartphone, or FarmVille on Facebook. Software developers have been able to expand rapidly into this arena by selling directly to the customer, bypassing the game publishing giants or traditional retail outlets.

Examining gender-specific concepts with regard to selling brings me straight back to the title of this book. It's the catch-22 of the world of marketing. The way forward is to take each brief, each client, as they come, and resist the temptation to follow what has worked before or rely on any clichés about what women want (boys, cake, shoes). The fact that this section is in here is enough to give me sleepless nights. Selling to females shouldn't be any different from selling to males, but it is. And here's the rub: just do something interesting, relevant and honest, and you might just slay the odd sacred cow.

are much more literate, and they tend to be more advanced readers and less physical, whereas young boys can be accessed better through humour as opposed to romance. Young boys don't respond to cute; young girls do. As a market researcher this is my bread and butter."

"When selling to females, it really depends on the context. There are no differences in some products and services, but huge disparities in others. For example, I don't think Apple really differentiates – although you could argue that its whole design ethos is feminized – but car manufacturers, for example, really continue to segment. Guess which approach I think will define the future…"

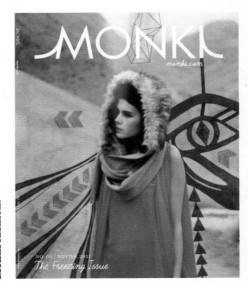

Beautiful youth: Crista Leonard's cover shot for Monki fashion.

34

Little Girl ad translation:

Headline: "Don't take the risk."

"With Europe's most punctual airline you can take care of all your meetings. Regardless of size. Book at sas.se"

"The difference between selling to males and females depends a bit on product and category but, generally, gender characteristics (usually culturally constructed) are subject to change – and strong advertising often leverages on and catalyses change. We are moving towards an age in which it is probably more relevant to look into interest spheres, social standing and education level than strictly gender. Herein lies an opportunity to make a product-benefit relevant – for example, Scandinavian Airlines' strategic communication focuses on punctuality, which is summarized as 'Take care of your time', showing how this benefits both men and women who are striving for a work/life balance. Gender roles are a fact, but they are constantly evolving. They can rapidly become outdated. Just look at an advertising strategy book from the 1950s, when selling strategies towards women stemmed from the suggestion that all they dreamt of was to get married and be a housewife."

35

Fashion truly is an interesting platform from which to nurture talent. This talent doesn't have to be directly involved with garment design – there is a lot of other content that needs to be produced for a brand. BLK DNM is an online-driven fashion house based in downtown New York. It does not conform to fashion seasons, and new items are launched when they are ready, which is something that marks it out as individual – a good starting point in the fashion game, especially for the youth.

Through its online presence (web/blog/Facebook app) BLK DNM hosts a channel of fashion, art, film and music, all recent and supported by the brand. All this talent and imagery is wrapped up in a printed publication called Gazette, which is the brand's main piece of advertising. This is an interesting proposition; not only does it promote the brand, but it also promotes the talent. It is something to pick up and read; a rare thing in these days of online media. The art direction of Gazette is killer.

"Women constantly look for inspiration and we are trying to respond to this by communicating a clearly defined BLK DNM look that always stays fresh. Men, on the other hand, generally stick to their favourite pieces, such as the perfect jeans/T-shirt/biker jacket. So, in addition to looks, we also offer a selection of essentials that can be bought as staple items and will always be available.

We are trying to create a brand with more depth and content. We want BLK DNM to be part of a new era with more conscious values: a luxury product at an accessible price, a direct conversation between the brand and the consumer, a culture based on creativity and collaboration, and the premise is to give something back to a cause that we care about. The aesthetic is inspired by our own intuition and taste rather than seasonal themes."

This campaign just blew me away. It was the
freshest thing I'd seen in ages – it had a tactile,
analogue bit of freshness in a digital world. And
it's from Mozambique!

36 **Mozambique Fashion Week**

37

In the West, culture and consumption have begun to merge and become one thing. A lot of people who believe they are contributing to subcultures or street culture are not involved in anything other than consumerism – but more about that later. The question here is: how do the youth consume musical content?

The digital revolution has had an enormous effect on the price of music (and films), reducing them as much as 90 per cent, which in turn affects the production of content. Music in some ways has become digital fodder, or noise that is used to fill in the spaces. In mainstream advertising this is nearly always the case. In other ways, the content created by brands has become as important and even more relevant to the lives of the youth than the (often) outdated content on TV.

The Internet has changed advertising, but it has blown apart how music is sold and consumed. Music was once a monopoly tightly controlled by a few major labels, but it has been democratized and taken over by the consumer. It used to be a high-value commodity for fans, and if you wanted to make an album it cost a lot of money and required a lot of effort. And talent. These days anyone can make music on his or her home PC or bedroom laptop, put it out and almost instantly get feedback on their blog, but I don't think it takes the same amount of effort. The more effort you put into something, the more you value it.

"Youth buys faces,
youth buys into itself,
youth buys utopia then turns it into dystopia,
because it cannot succeed purely on youth,
old age wants to buy youth,
and it can but it also cannot,
because old age has a conscience and carries a guilt trip,
whereas youth does not.
I don't know what the hell I'm talking about
but I'm thinking about Apple, the Beatles shop in Baker Street,
designed by the fool because it was a poem.
It's 12.29 a.m. Saturday October 1st 2011,
sorry, I'm tired and I'm also an idiot, good night.'

Music used to define who you were. Nowadays the music industry is way down the careers list for most kids, and has been overtaken by the games and technology industries. When I was a kid I had to mission to buy a record or see a band. Those records I still have today and they all tell a story. Today a lot of people download MP3s and never listen to them.

Despite this, music is still a vital element of youth advertising – it is the soundtrack to a million ads, and it represents youth in a way that only music can. It's the stuff you can't bottle. Music has the power to touch our very souls, seamlessly linking the message with the medium, the concept with the output; it helps create the magic that rolls over into a sale. Music is an immensely powerful force when used correctly in marketing, and this is why brands and advertisers are so keen to create relationships with musicians and producers. Royalties from adverts, virals, YouTube and apps such as Spotify have become an important revenue source for labels. At one time, it was not easy to convince a legendary band to allow their music to be used in a commercial, but things are different now. Iggy Pop appearing in an online insurance ad is a prime example of how it has changed. TV spots have always had a major effect on what we listen to, but now brands such as Heineken are using them to break new acts in return for usage rights. What goes around comes around, I guess. In 2008 Groove Armada, the

"There is the consumer's point of view and then there is the industry's. I think what has changed for the industry, is that maybe ten years ago we were focusing on our core product – CDs – and everything else was secondary. Now you need to try and monetize music in every way, not just the audio, but the product and artist too. From sync deals to brand partnerships to touring, it all matters, and all should enable us to see a return on investment. Labels and artists alike need to be looking at every aspect. For the consumers I think what has changed is that the music now comes in every possible format and price range (or for free, when downloading illegally). Digitally the options are numerous, but even vinyl is selling more again. And a lot of fans are buying into D2C (direct to consumer) products, where bands offer standard package deals (album with a T-shirt and/or a concert ticket) or unique experiences (have dinner with the band, go skydiving with an artist)."

British dance music duo, released music via the Bacardi brand and only played live at Barcardi-branded events. As part of the recording contract, the first between a band and a drinks brand, Bacardi funded the production of a four-track EP, which was then released digitally and in hard-copy format. The agreement also allowed Bacardi to commission tracks for use in advertising and other promotional campaigns.

The new model for breaking music has been exemplified by Odd Future Wolf Gang Kill Them All (OFWGKTA). The West Coast music, mayhem and skate crew at first gave their work away via their Tumblr site, using their own language and visual identity from day one, and creating their own musical genre that dared you to try and define it. But allegedly the whole campaign was being orchestrated from behind the scenes by one of the most prolific and clever minds in the music industry: Odd Future manager Christian Clancy. The one thing I know for sure is that Odd Future's video "Yonkers" (where member Tyler, the Creator, hangs himself at the end), and subsequent mental appearance on the Jimmy Fallon show (where Mr Fallon was holding up a QR code as he introduced them) had something to do with their blowing up. How could you not pay attention?

"Someone once said to me that 'labels focus on songs that sound like hits, not feel like hits'. [With Odd Future] every decision we make is based on what's authentic to them. They are who they are. They turn down covers 'cos they don't read the magazine. I love that. These kids are smarter than the music that's being sold to them. If kids like it then they will find it out. If they connect on an emotional level, then kids will go to the seven different sites it takes to find one answer."

Consumption in full effect.

"The primary focus is now on getting the word of the band out there in every possible way, connecting to people and building a fan base, and getting them to engage with the band in whichever way; even if they are downloading the record illegally, they still might go to a concert, buy a T-shirt, etc. And most labels are now in a 360° partnership with artists, and share revenues when it comes to live shows and merchandise as well. It's up to us to find out how fans are willing to 'buy' into a band, and fulfil that demand. That is a major shift: instead of making a lot of money mainly selling CDs, it's about making a little bit in a lot of different ways."

"Everyone thinks it was hard work, but we have connections to powerful people. Odd Future is just a big gimmick, and it's working…"

38

James Hilton started AKQA after becoming
disillusioned with art school. It's a good job
he did, as AKQA has gone on to create some
groundbreaking work and has been instrumental
in blurring the boundaries between content and
communication, which is no small feat.

"Back in the day when we started out, and I was
still statistically young, we had two things that
we asked: 'So what?' and 'What's in it for me?' –
these are the two questions that anyone will say
when presented with something. You have to find
out the motivations for 'So what?' and the benefits
for 'What's in it for me?' And that's all it is really.
Make people's lives more fun, less complex and
less cluttered. Be a positive addition to society."

Analogue or digital?

"It's kind of laughable that people still use terms
like 'digital'. I suppose as soon as you give
something a term it becomes comfortable and
understandable, it becomes a medium to master.
You should be concentrating on mastering the
communication, not the medium; be effective,
not digital. Audiences have been brought up
with all this shit advertising around them – I don't
even watch TV any more, because I can't stand it.

I get so irritated by adverts that are, in the main, appalling, but – and this is what really sets me off – they're also louder than the TV programme I'm watching. Maybe that's just me getting old and cantankerous, but I find that intellectually insulting, and so does my 15-year-old niece. She asked me, 'Why do they turn up the TV ads? They're already shit, so they're just making them shitter.' Which is an astonishingly good point; 15-year-olds are, on the whole, interested in the things around them. They seek out brands that are interesting and want to change stuff. So clearly more effort is required of brands and their agencies to focus on this and a whole lot less on trying to talk like the kids, innit. Because there is way too much of that already."

How do you connect to the youth?

"A worryingly large proportion of marketers and brands massively underestimate the intelligence

of youth. In terms of their levels of cultural and emotional intelligence, and just plain savviness, there has never been a generation like it. I'm sure this is due to the biblical scale of sensory input they are exposed to every single second of every single day. It's turned them into amazing curators, because if they actually took all of this noise in, they'd go mad, so they have to edit their lives to only the wavelength of information they want coming through.

I hate the way marketers talk down to the youth or try to talk their language. It's just embarrassing when brands use what they think is youth-speak in advertising, as usually it's either totally out of context or simply inaccurate. Most of the kids out there don't even speak the way advertisers think. There is a great quote, that I'm going to get totally wrong, about youth: 'They stand around on street corners, they conceal their faces, they intimidate people and they don't listen to their elders, they don't pay attention at school, they're rude, they're uncouth and they rebel against their parents. It wasn't like that in my day.' This was written by a monk in the 15th century. Attitudes and people don't change; the way adults look at the youth will never change. As a species we haven't evolved in 200,000 years, but our ability to process input has increased substantially. Generally, though, we still want the same stuff we did way back then: for things to be better, less complicated and more fun, and the youth are no different. They don't want the bullshit getting in the way of having a good time. They have their sphere of enjoyment and from time to time will explore outside of this world. Over time this exploration grows – this is, after all, the joy of expanding experiences. The young generation aren't interested if a brand plops itself outside of their world and announces that its stuff is better. The youth's response is that they are quite comfortable where they are, and

iPad app. Get shopping.

if the brand wants to engage with them then it should come into their world, on their terms, and amplify stuff that they are already doing. Ultimately, it is 'Make what we're doing better.'"

How do you cope with difficult clients?

"As a general rule we collaborate with our clients, as the best work is only possible with what I call 'the art of good parenting'. An idea is like a child you bring up; if you have one dysfunctional and one functional parent then you're gonna get a fucked-up kid. It's the same for an idea – you need two good parents. You need excited and engaged clients as well as agencies. The bottom line is that clients only ever get the work they deserve; you can be the most amazing agency or client on the planet, but if one of you doesn't give a shit then it will show in the work. I look back at the work we've done here at AKQA and without doubt the best is the result of an inspiring

relationship with the client. It goes back to the
'So what?' and 'What's in it for me?' questions,
and the surgical strike of a solution that does one
thing amazingly well: communicating straight
into the soul of the audience. If you have to
educate your client, that's just part of the job. It
might mean you have to take incremental steps
to slowly get to the place you want to be, but our
duty of care to our clients is to give them the best
work possible for their brand. Part of that duty of
care is also to ensure that we're the right agency
for them. If it ever gets to a point where we can't
behave and create in the way we wish, we either
have to recalibrate the relationship or call it a day.
That's best for everyone, and as long as you're
professional and grown-up about it, you can do it
without sacrificing future relationships."

39

Nike True City was the game-changing iPhone app that literally transformed the travel-writing industry overnight. It certainly opened my eyes to what it was now possible to do with a smartphone, Wi-Fi, and some quality, up-to-date cultural currency. And all this from a sports brand?

"True City never came out of a brief – it was born out of AKQA. As we deal so much with Nike, we are good friends with all of Nike's influencers – street influences, artists, musicians, people like that. And we've got offices all over the world and come from all over the world, and like to visit each other's cities. But the question is, what do I do when I get there? Unless I'm with a local I'm a bit lost. I could buy a *Time Out* or *Lonely Planet.* How do you become a local? How do you avoid looking like a tourist? I hate looking like a tourist. If I need a map I'll take a photo of it and put it on my iPhone so I don't walk around looking like a mugging target. We wanted to use all this stuff so that people could visit cities and not feel like tourists – how can we give them the hidden places? The idea of True City was to reveal the hidden – all the stuff you wouldn't know unless you lived there. It was a cool *Lonely Planet.* So we used all our connections and took it to Nike, and they liked it, but weren't that sure about it

– they are a sports-apparel business, so they were into all the influences but weren't that sure about the validity of what was essentially a travel app. But we secured a bit of a budget to do a test case and we did London first – it was a huge success. This opened the floodgates, and then everybody wanted to jump on. Paris. Amsterdam. Berlin. And there were user-page calls for us to come to their city. The test case for me was when I went to Paris with my girlfriend with True City on my phone and I literally had the best week in Paris that I've ever had. Suddenly I knew where to go – bars, restaurants, trainers shops. I was like the bees knees that week and it was all down to True City. Before you go to a new city you call around all your mates and find out where to go, all the little gems, but you need to aggregate all that stuff, and how do you keep it live?

Keeping it live with
Nike True City.

The Internet facilitates a two-way conversation between brand and public like never before. These days, a brand can't just yell at you from a TV screen while you passively absorb its attempts at manipulation. Now, it has to address you as an equal. That's particularly pertinent for 'youth advertising'. Brands like Nike may still be semi-religions for their target group, but the likes of Wayne Rooney also have to get down from their pulpit now and again, and mingle with us mere mortals. The Internet is the democratization of capitalism."

MINI Getaway is a real-time game played in both
the digital and analogue worlds, created by Jung
von Matt, Sweden, which takes the idea of a
traditional board game and runs with it (literally).

A city near you becomes a digital/analogue game board.

"We were asked by MINI to create an idea to launch the all-new MINI Countryman. The idea should engage people on multiple levels: physically, emotionally and socially. The idea of making the streets of Stockholm a living game board for the world's biggest reality game on iPhone came up early in the process, but the challenge was how to maintain people's interest over a two-week period.

The main goal was to create MINI evangelists in Sweden. We knew that we were on to something out of the ordinary, and our hopes were high, but the result exceeded our expectations, with followers from over ninety countries and players spending an average of five hours and six minutes running up and down the streets of Stockholm, trying to catch the virtual MINI (which means interacting with the brand). MINI doubled its sales over the following six-month period and a year later had maintained that sales volume – an all-time high.

We recently launched MINI Getaway in Tokyo – a game board thirty times bigger than Stockholm. The engagement was astounding. The total distance over which the gamers hunted the car was equivalent to 120 laps around the world, or more than six round trips to the moon. The car was won by 22-year-old Joel, who gamed in team with his dad."

41

I'm always keen to dispel myths, as they usually are just clichés in disguise, so perhaps sex doesn't sell. Ethically, I'm not sure if it's OK for brands or businesses to use sex to move stock. It's an easy, no-risk way to grab attention, but after you've dealt with all the social and political connotations, and you've caught the audience's eye – is it worth it? I'm not sure it is. What connects the youth to a brand using sex in their adverts? I think perhaps it's the human truth behind how it makes them feel; the animal instincts deep within. It will work if the youth can identify with a geek looking at the smoking-hot boy/girl, and the story you're telling is how they don't have a hope in hell of actually pulling the hottie, rather than just using somebody with a perfect face and fantastic physique in your ad because he/she

is attractive and that is it. When you don't have the looks, the money, the fame (i.e. us normal mortals), you're going to have to dig deep to step up and pull a member of the opposite sex – and humour works every time. That's what the youth relate to, male or female. There have to be ads where they go, "Yeah, that's true."

The youth of today see through the bullshit quickly. There is a very clear distinction in their minds between commercial propaganda, and advertising that's a little more bespoke for their generation. They will still be aware that there's a brand behind it, but they understand the brand has gone to some trouble, and sometimes, because of this, they might anoint your brand as cool.

"Yes, sex definitely sells. There was a study done by researchers at Yale in collaboration with advertising creatives that was presented at Cannes Lions. The goal was to see if they could influence monkey behaviour with advertising. The results of the study showed that the primates really loved pictures of their alpha males … as well as genitals. The researchers believe this shows that two things drive purchasing habits: sex and celebrity. What we can categorically conclude from this study is this: if we had cast Lady Gaga and President Obama in our Skittles spot it would have received at least twice the number of hits."

"Of course sex works – sex is a prime mover, an absolute trigger – but I think the youth see it coming if it's too blatant. I was asked very recently to talk at my son's (all boys) school about sexism in advertising. And here you had all these testosterone-filled boys watching as I'd flick up some very overtly sexual images for tight underpants or push-up bras, and they kind of got it but they wanted more. We had an interesting debate when we put up the Old Spice (Mustafa) ad; he's a good-looking guy saying you can't look like me, but you can smell like me, and the boys loved the idea. Everyone likes the concept of being attractive to the opposite sex, and sex is going to sell, but sex with a bit of humour, sex with a smile. TBWA sold a hell of a lot of Wonderbras with 'Hello Boys' – sex with humour. People react much more when it's not just below-the-belt raw sex, and it has something more. Even sex with a slight poignancy, if that's necessary.

Stuff that is more like visual pornography is good for a snigger and *FHM*, but I don't think you can build a brand on it. AXE [LYNX in the UK] is very clever, as it's absolute sex but with a bit of a chuckle. Sex is always going to sell, but I think you have to smooth it out rather than lay it out, as after you've done the shocking, in your face, you've nowhere else to go – after the money shot."

Sex sells for this Shanghai skater.

42

The second short-cut to grabbing attention is fame. Famous faces instantly attract the eye, and sometimes this is a hard proposition to ignore. I'm not really that much of a fan of the sex and celebrity routes, but I'm not stupid either – a sale is a sale is a sale. However, in all honesty, I do think the kind of advertising content produced using famous faces is pretty terrible, often coming low on the creative scale. A client who insists on selling off the back of the famous is one you could do without, as at some point this is going to come back to bite you. Fame is never a substitute for quality, or a good idea.

The other side of the coin is that when you're talking about celebrity, you're actually talking about recognition and self-expression, and there are a lot of things in and around this area through which brands can help people create the connections to express things that are important to them. Whether it's an academic, social or professional achievement, the concept of fame can be so much more than "This singer likes this soda – why shouldn't you!" This worked in an era when advertising was about telling stories, and these days there is still an interest among consumers about what famous people are doing – but the trick (if you go down the celebrity route) is to make the communication authentic, not contrived.

"[Fame and celebrity] are real cultural means that will exist for quite some time. These are basic human motivators. Advertising has played into both the positives and negatives for years, with positive and negative promises made about products. But with the rise of social media, celebrities are now talking to their fans in a totally different way, and people like Gaga and Justin Bieber are building legitimate connections. They have been pulled into advertising here and there, and some celebrities have stepped away as they've felt the taint, but now they are not forced to participate in one single way. They can have a proper connection without the hard sell. The shift of marketing broadly is towards authenticity – it's OK to make a statement or promise, if you as a brand or business can actually back it up."

43

Mandi Lennard – London fashion publicist extraordinaire – has been keeping Barbie's cutting edge sharp for a while now, and in 2011 she helped take her out east to London's most fashionable hair salon, BLEACH.

In October 2010, hair stylist Alex Brownsell and her business partner Samantha Teasdale launched their first salon in Dalston. Since then, platinum silver, recession roots, dip dye, pastel highlights and rainbow hair have been readily embraced by the industry. From Hollywood to Hackney, BLEACH's clients have included Florence Welch, M.I.A., Pixie Geldof and Sky Ferreira, among many others. Alex created eight looks for Barbie, including how she is dressed.

But this project isn't just something to read about online or in the fashion mags – there is a great digital-to-analogue transition that makes this piece of communication so strong. By using an online program and your own inkjet printer, Barbie Design Printables allows you to print directly onto personalized clip-in hair extensions, with any colours or designs you like. In one fell swoop Lennard and BLEACH have taken Barbara Millicent Roberts (aka Barbie) to another level of hip. And image making. And PR. This could be a glimpse into the future of advertising.

"Since 1959, Barbie has been recognized as the original teenage fashion model. In the past fifty years, she has established herself as one of the world's leading fashion icons. She's been dressed by a whole host of designers including Prada, Burberry, Chanel, Roksanda Ilincic and Danielle Scutt. She first broke the plastic ceiling in the 1960s when, as an astronaut, she went to space four years before man walked on the moon. In the 1980s she took to the boardroom as 'Day to Night' CEO Barbie, just as women began to break into management. And in the 1990s, she ran for President, before any female candidate ever made it onto the presidential ballot. At any given moment in the past fifty years, Barbie has been a reflection of the times and is culturally relevant."

"Barbie was the first person I experimented on when I was a kid, and now having the opportunity for her to be our client at BLEACH is incredible. Her design-able hair is a genius concept that has also inspired some new creations inside the salon!"

44

As with the moving image, the photo is one of the key ingredients for effective and genuine youth advertising. There are some exceptions – moving ads, animation, etc. – but one thing I've noticed is that a lot of the great youth ads are based on or around a photo. Capturing that moment, distilling the essence of youth onto a page or screen, means that at first glance the ad appears authentic. This doesn't necessarily mean it will work, as you have to get the rest of the elements exactly right, but it's a vital first step: your foot in the door. This means you have to employ a new breed of photographer, one who understands the youth and is probably young themselves. This may present something of a problem, as agencies and brands are always edgy about what they see as taking a risk with unknown or unproven talents; however, I think it is riskier to use an established/safe photographer who will deliver something that doesn't connect to the audience.

The photographers featured here are all bright young talents who – in my opinion – are able to capture and distil the look and feel of youth.

"To see the youngster soul, see your inner youngster. I believe that authentic photographs are made like this, by giving your soul in that moment."

"With night vision and a steady aim, a good shot of the youth should be open to interpretation, a reflection of a transitional state. The best way to connect to youth is by association with trends."

"I don't have special thoughts while I'm shooting. Being young, you must feel the pain, so pain can make me feel the sense of existence. If you think I take these photos because I'm obsessed with youth, I'd rather say I really enjoy the pleasure of pain and dependence on the sense of existence."

Ren Hang captures Chinese youth.

"I'm not 45 years old, I'm 22, and I feel the same as my generation, who are depressed and in alcoholic states of consciousness. I was very lucky that I caught a wave. I was working in the best club in Moscow – that was only the beginning. It was like something in Studio 54: creative, insane, the best of the best, in one place. I knew everyone there and they all trusted me. I work with subtle matter. When I click the button, I capture not only what I see, but also what I feel at that moment. In all my work there is something more than just a snapshot of a man, and that is a mirror of his soul."

"I don't think I have a predefined approach towards photographing youth. However, they do tend to have something special to offer at this age in which they expose their personality in a mixture of challenge and vulnerability."

Crista Leonard submerges fashion.

"Be involved. Don't stand at the sideline with your camera in hand waiting for something to happen. Be part of the moment. As a photographer you have licence to be a part of things that otherwise would be off limits. The camera isn't just a camera; it's a universal passport, entry ticket and AAA pass to experiences. My images are as much about me as they are the subjects in the frame. I'm never really trying to capture someone else's life, just parts of my own with people I meet along the way."

"It seems to me, when shooting young people, they have so much innate personality and style, the best thing one can do is shoot them as they are."

Natasha Bonner shoots the landscape of youth.

"A good youth portrait has a nice mixture of confidence, vulnerability and naivety. Advertisers need to keep things real and genuine. Youth cultures are wearing their hearts on their sleeves and can sniff out the fakes right away. Use real people, real locations; if not, it's just a facade and you might as well advertise using cartoon characters."

"Youth is fascinating because it is a very intense period of your life, one in which you really do live every moment in the present, one in which your friends become your new family, teaching each other the freedom of independence and the exhilaration of being alive. I think many artists try to capture that 'breathless excitement' and intense self-awareness that seem to go hand in hand with youth, that feeling that age and time will never touch you, you are untouchable."

South African youth by Jono.

"I started shooting with altruistic intentions: I was going to give the nightlife a face, show that my little city, Port Elizabeth, had a pulse. The youth here are insanely complacent – when something does happen they don't want to go, and then they complain that nothing ever happens here, which is a lie. I've found that a positive, professional attitude and a lot of luck have aided me in securing some amazing work. At the end of the day a talent or a skill will only take you so far before your laurels give way and you fall on your ass. So, where my work has found a home is with the people I take pride in shooting. I have endeavoured to maintain as much of a professional outlook as possible. Being on time and presentable doesn't hurt; you can have fun and still produce something tangible for a market that wants to see its own face in the end product."

45

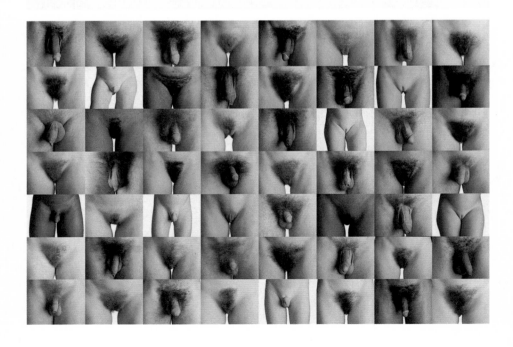

One of the greatest campaigns in youth advertising was the work created and photographed by Oliviero Toscani when he was creative director of Benetton. Although this has been very well documented, it is still vitally important and comes from a body of work by one of the true geniuses of advertising.

When Oliviero joined the company, Benetton's clothes were on a par with a middle-class brand such as M&S or Bloomingdale's – the opposite of a youth brand – but the power of the advertising made them great. This is one of those rare times when a single man with a vision has really made something happen. He was in complete creative control and even shot the ads himself.

Oliviero is a living embodiment of rebellion and youthful spirit, which is so important to keep alive, especially if you want to connect to the youth. We spent some time together in a Roman traffic jam…

How do you think brands connect with the youth?

"Brands always hope to connect to the youth, but they rarely do, as it's not easy. If you want to attach your brand successfully to the youth, then you have to ignore the marketing people. Actually, you should never go with what marketing is telling you, it's a big mistake. You cannot just try to infiltrate the youth and its subculture. The only way is if you have the courage and strength to make an experiment, create something amazing, and then the youth might follow you, but only if you take them on an adventurous trip. Advertising agencies can't even get close to what the youth are thinking, because of their structure, their way of thinking, their research – it's all bullshit! You have to invent something alternative, something revolutionary, to make the youth interested in your brand."

45   172   **Interview with a legend:**   ↓   **Oliviero Toscani**
                             Oliviero Toscani

Have you ever had a brand moment that has stayed with you?

"There was very little advertising when I was young, but what struck me the most was when I used to go with my father, in the early 1950s, to the Piazza del Duomo in Milan, and we would see the advertising in neon lights in the evening. Flashing on and off. It was like the youth spirit – it was light and energetic. I didn't even care about the product, that wasn't the point. Aesthetically it was all about the flashing coloured lights – there was no LED back then. They also wrote the news on the wall like that. It is something that deep down appeals to the child inside every human being, just like when you walk in Times Square today, or years ago in Piccadilly. Everything is oversized, you feel like a child, and it's magical, it's like being in a theatrical environment. Young people especially like that – almost like being in a night club."

**When you were working on the Benetton campaigns,
were you targeting the youth?**

"My work is always for the young spirit, for sure.
My Anorexia campaign was aimed at the young.
I also did a campaign for road safety, as young
people think they are immortal; they have a totally
different relationship to life and death. When you're
40 or 50 you begin to think that you may die, but
young people never even think it's possible to
die. However, they are very sensitive to scars and
getting their faces mutilated in a car accident. I did
a campaign to promote wearing safety belts and
crash helmets, as it wasn't mandatory back then.
It was based on the fact that you might mutilate
your face; I never talked about dying. Now, if you
are young, you can have sex and die young.

All my communication is for the young spirit.
You have to understand that there is a difference
between youth as a young spirit and youth as
an age. There are some people who are in their

A 1972 ad for B+B Italia. The sofa has been in continuous production ever since.

thirties, forties, fifties, sixties, who are much younger than people who are in their twenties. The whole perception of youth has changed a lot. When I was really young there was no such thing as youth. It wasn't invented with my generation. I'm 70 next year; I was 18 in 1960, like the Beatles. Before us, there wasn't any youth generation. We became powerful because we were the first generation with a little money in our pockets, so a market was developed, for records, etc. We had enough money to change the market, and so then came the youth marketing. Nowadays youth marketing is all about speculation."

46

Corporate responsibility or, in other words, doing good. The "star maker" syndrome of selling instant fame and money is dead; long live the community. One of the best ways for a brand to move forward is to do something that makes a difference. It is becoming increasingly important for brands to acknowledge a responsibility for all aspects of society, and the question is: how long will it be before they take this seriously?

In some ways I think that corporate responsibility could be the crucial difference in the land of marketing, and not just another box to tick. It is easy to be cynical and scathing about massive brands doing good work – these corporations have never really cared much about the planet or about communities, and now they are suddenly showing a responsible side. On the other hand, some initiatives can make a difference, and consumers are smart enough to punish companies that don't embrace corporate responsibility, by voicing distrust and, most effectively, by not buying.

It's hard to separate people from their money, but it becomes a lot easier if you can give them a great product, service or ethos that makes them want to spend – for example, by doing some good work that actually means something to the people you're talking to. The youth are smart and will discover the truth about whatever product you're trying to sell with a couple of mouse

"If we teach our children about hygiene, if we teach our children about nutrition, and safety, and sexuality, then shouldn't we also be teaching our children to be responsible consumers? Since so much of our advertising is focused on the youth, don't you think we as a culture need to educate these kids about what advertising is, and to see it for what it is? I think we should have media education in our elementary schools. But corporate responsibility is just another form of advertising. The advertising vehicles of the 20th century – print and broadcast media – are not as powerful as they used to be, so finding a way to engage with the public is part of what these responsibilities are, and good works are a way of doing this, just in the same way that the royal family does good work as part of their PR campaign for the House of Windsor."

clicks, so trying to bullshit them is only going to reinforce the idea that all advertising people are dishonest. You actually have to get out there and do something for the wider good.

In the last ten years there has been a surge in large brands appearing to do the right thing. Perhaps it is because those brands have found a conscience, or perhaps it's because they have no choice but to do what is now expected of them. Whatever the reason, the result is that they get out and spend some of their money doing something for the good of the world, which is what we need more of. There is huge scope for this in the youth market, as it is a rapidly expanding demographic. It's crucial for brands to show the youth that they care about them, their communities, and their lives. I mean actually demonstrating this, not just talking the talk.

Projects like Orange RockCorps (a "pro-social production company"), Pepsi Refresh (trading a multimillion-dollar Super Bowl commercial for a $20 million social campaign) and Levi's We Are Workers (Levi's donating $1 million for the "reinvention" of the US town of Braddock, PA) are all great examples of how brands can not only plough some much-needed cash into communities and causes, but also engage the youth to care about something a bit more meaningful, and get them involved in social projects.

"Brands can't buy respectability, or indeed somehow hoodwink people into believing that they care. The important thing is always authenticity. And being genuine. And in more circumstances than I care to mention, brands very often start to get involved in things that audiences feel are way beyond them."

A building-sized miner in Jo'burg from the Anglo American campaign "Real Mining. Real People. Real Difference".

From a newborn in a clinic in Mali to the fields of Afghanistan, corporate responsibility has to have a global reach.

"Corporate responsibility is noteworthy, since advertising aims to change behaviours in a given way, and holistically a more sustainable behaviour is, of course, one of the most important objectives. Well-executed advertising often results in increased sales, which in turn can mean exploitation of resources as well as increased waste, since products are being consumed or becoming obsolete. But a lot of people are interested in how corporations act in a world with many challenges. Therefore, it is interesting to talk about how corporations relate to and take responsibility for the impact they have on natural and social resources. If a company can have their marketing budgets contribute to a better world through brand-building projects with a higher benefit than just brand-building, advertising has a great opportunity that needs to be seized."

"Most large firms have corporate responsibility initiatives. Corporations are part of society and thus they should take responsibility for their actions as part of their 'social contract' and try to behave as ethically as possible. Initiatives like this are more often about environment and work conditions, etc., and how a brand can improve or at least reduce the harm of doing business. This is, of course, brand-building, but shouldn't be seen as advertising, which is more about creating brand-image and desire for a brand's product. Blurring these two lines is dishonest, because the objective of these two initiatives is not about the greater good, but about building the brand. This isn't totally clear in some campaigns."

47

Waves for Water is a unique social project sponsored by surf brand Hurley. Their mission is simple: to get clean water to people who need it.

The goal is to take portable water filters into countries around the world. There are different options for each region, based on needs in various areas – they range from ceramic filters that can be transported by one person, to larger filters that can provide clean water to an entire village. As a sister project, water-based brand Hurley has developed a DIY volunteer programme called Clean Water Couriers, in which surfers searching for waves in third world countries carry filters with them in their luggage, pack a few filters in their suitcase and either connect with local non-profit organizations in that area or personally travel to villages to set them up. Creating these filtration systems is simple: generally all you need are paint buckets (easily found in any country), a knife to make a hole, spigots, and ceramic-drip water filters that can be purchased for $25 each or the preferred community filter at $50.

"People living in impoverished areas die every day from drinking dirty water. While having access to clean water is a luxury that many of us take for granted, there are millions living in nations with no filtration systems in place. Kids drink from the same streams where animals bathe. In addition, there's no clean water available for surgery if someone is injured, putting the wounded at risk of deathly infection. Contaminated water kills 3.3 million people each year. Every fifteen seconds, a child dies from water-related diseases.

We always feel good about giving the gift of clean water. In my opinion, water is a God-given right, like air. But the fact that there are still such staggering statistics – such as that one in six people do not have access to clean drinking water – means there is obviously a hole in the equation. I say it all the time, but there is absolutely no reason why ANYONE should die from dirty water when solutions like these simple filtration

An Afghan woman gets to grips with a Waves for Water filter.

devices exist. So our primary goal has been to fill that hole by simply connecting the brilliant technology with the people who need it. It's nobody's fault, there are just missing links in the chain sometimes. In this case, the gifted minds who created this incredible technology did their job perfectly – they created user-friendly devices that can make almost any contaminated water drinkable. But it isn't necessarily their job to identify the individuals around the world who so desperately need them…or be the ones to deliver them, for that matter. And the folks around the world who are in such dire need don't have the slightest idea that these solutions exist. That's where we come in…and on behalf of Waves for Water I will say we are honoured to play a role, of any size, in the big vision that so many people around the world share, which is: clean water for everyone."

I flew out to Mali to document the work that the Only The Brave Foundation had been doing in the village of Dioro. The OTB Foundation was founded by Only The Brave Group, which includes brands such as Diesel, 55DSL, Maison Martin Margiela and Viktor & Rolf. Dioro is an hour's drive from the city of Ségou, and five hours from the capital, Bamako. I was there to shoot moving and still images that would then be used to document and spread the word about the project. One of the ways this was going to be presented was through an online virtual world that would replicate the real village and connect it with the youth of the world, which I thought was a pretty cool way to get people interested in something they'd usually ignore.

I was a bit cynical about the project (I thought it was all about selling denim) until I got out there and witnessed at first hand just how much the foundation had achieved: it had built a school, a medical centre, a solar-powered Internet centre, and helped to create a system of clean water for homes. Meeting and greeting, interviewing and shooting the locals, I began to understand how brands could make a difference in the daily lives of people who really need help. This does not have to roll over directly into sales, but it can build the social standing of the brand, which is more valuable in the long term. This goes back to the idea of brands becoming involved in the communities and lives of the youth, in more than just product placement.

"I created the Only The Brave Foundation to contribute to sustainable development. And when we sat down to choose where to focus our efforts, we decided to start with Africa, a continent that has the resources and the capacity – it only needs the opportunity. I visited Mali and the village we support there last year, and I was touched not only by the progress of the village itself but also by the incredible richness of traditions, history, know-how and hope for the future I sensed there. Helping Africans educate themselves, improve their skills, and have access to training and initial investment to start businesses is fundamental to get them out of the poverty circle and build the basis for their future and the future of their countries. This is why we are working alongside the local population in different sectors (agriculture, health, education, infrastructure and business development), sharing with them all the necessary knowledge to build or restructure infrastructure, to create

The most difficult thing for the foundation was to make sure that the money was spent for the good of the people – that it actually made it to the poor. There is always a danger, when pouring foreign money into developing countries, that the funds will get diluted on the way, but I was surprised to see that the OTB Foundation had a firm grip on exactly how, why and when the money got used. This is one of the benefits of organizations and foundations like this – they are not part of an NGO or aid programme or charity, and so there is less red tape to cut through to make sure the money gets spent properly.

or develop businesses, etc. We are not doing things for them, but with them. Only in this way can true, sustainable development be guaranteed."

Authentic faces of corporate responsibility in action.

Converse poster by Raul Urias.

I love both advertising and art, and often have the Warholian problem of distinguishing which is which. As much as it is hated by artists and activists around the world, advertising has become a great place for young, mainly urban, artists to work and make money doing what they love. It stops them having to get a shitty McJob to pay the bills, which is so important in the development of fresh talent. In the old days all marketing was considered the work of the devil and any self-respecting artist would never be seen to be doing ad work, although Toulouse-Lautrec, Dalí and Warhol all churned out advertising. Now that the consumer is king and there is such a mass of imagery, info, movies, art and words all vying for our attention, advertising is an acceptable way of getting some much-needed publicity if you are an artist.

There is a small group of artists around the world whose style, ethos and choices ensure that their work is always spot on for advertising, and always connects to the youth. This is something incredible to behold and is vitally important in the search to discover what really works in youth advertising: show, don't tell! Youth advertising has a massive audience, and, as with photography, if the artist chooses to go down that route, they can reach a lot of people very quickly.

"Advertising searches to do the same things as art and art often searches to do the same things as advertising. That's always been the horror show of what people call the postmodern world."

"When I get a commission I do not really think much about whether the design is targeted for youth or not. Most of the time agencies commission me to work for a product because they feel my work can speak the same language their target speaks, so most of the time I'm asked to 'do what you like/know what to do'. So, thinking about my way of approaching youth in my work…I simply follow my instincts and, to get closer to them, I try to break some rules from time to time."

"I think youth advertising has varying levels of success. Maybe its success is dependent upon how 'real' it is. If it's fake you can spot it a mile off. I've made some money from youth advertising,

but unfortunately I think by the time advertising agencies or PR or marketing companies get their hands on it, it's the beginning of the end for a movement. That seems to be the way of things. The money takes over, the soul is sucked out of it, and it makes way for something new. I think it's most effective when they just let artists do what they do. Although there have been a number of occasions when I've thought, 'I can't believe we are being paid to do this!'"

"I didn't think too much. I thought it would be cool to draw an image that is really straightforward, like the 1970s cigarette ads, where you just see a guy smokes and he got all the bitches; it's that simple. So that was pretty much what I had in mind – cold vodka, hot girls…I also had this feeling I tried to capture, something that is hard to explain, it's that certain way you see lights sometimes when you're drunk, and all the colours just fit right.

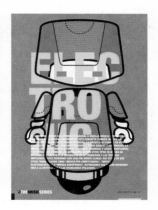

I don't know, normally I love acid colours that burn in the eye so this was a bit different…"

Unga's killer work for Stoli.

Advertising as art in action here, with some incredible work from LICHTFAKTOR, a collective of creatives from many different fields: graffiti writers, a coder, a graphic designer, a video artist, ballet dancers and jugglers. Every one is a specialist in his or her field. The one thing they have in common is that they all like to work with light, and they all learn from each other.

The images opposite show the work they created in collaboration with director Noah Harris, for TalkTalk, which was shot on the streets of Johannesburg.

"LICHTFAKTOR is a group of three individuals, but I think I can speak for all and say: YES. Every creative work, good idea, conversation, situation, interest, music, relationship, up and down shapes your art and understanding of things. I am a child of the 1970s; science fiction, comics, electronic music, film and art shaped me a lot, but also my school, it was a special school (Odenwaldschule) with the motto 'Become who you are' (*Werde der du bist*). Picasso was the first artist to use light-writing, but in photography you find many more people who did it. He combined two techniques: painting and photography.

We started this project in 2006, when we heard of 'light graffiti' for the first time. Apart from Picasso, we are inspired by Marko-93, PiKA PiKA, Blu, graffiti, street art, comics, visual music, Wolf Vostell, Stanley Kubrick, David Lynch, George Lucas, Oskar Fischinger, Laurie Anderson, daily life and the Internet, of course."

51

Illustration for MTV.
By Pomme Chan.

Does successful communication design have a look that appeals to the youth market? It does indeed, and although it's a bit like the title of this book, I want to show (not tell) how this is in reality. Over to the design talents of the world.

"We keep an eye on everything – we read magazines and weblogs, see exhibitions, hear music, we watch news as well as movies, we talk, we listen to others, we study, we eat organic food and water the plants, we travel, we see other cultures, other colours, other compositions, we dance, laugh and have fun. Mix all that together...*voilà*!"

"My little sister makes awesome self-portraits – that appeals to me. I like M/M Paris, art/vertising. I like my friend Kaspar, who draws big ugly faces and then pastes them up around my area, turning beige suburbia into something colourful and interesting. Boo to the governing bodies of Barcelona who are taking away the colour of that once fine city. Valparaíso, Chile – now that is a place with some great street art. They even use sticks and stones in their work. Sustainable Chilean street art. Three cheers for them."

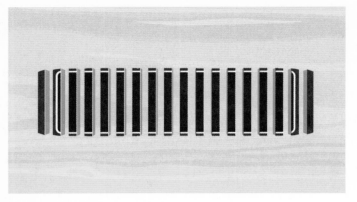

Artwork from Nokia BlackBox exhibition by Roy Poh / A Beautiful Design, Singapore.

"In the late 1990s and early 2000s, as a young aspiring designer, I was like a sponge, soaking up art, fashion, design, photography, wherever I could find it. The Internet wasn't the source, though; I would sit in magazine shops for hours on end culling through every avant-garde magazine I could get my hands on. We (RoAndCo) have been fortunate to have our work published on some really great design blogs as well as in a handful of graphic-design books and magazines, which I find is our way of connecting with a young audience. If Pulp can be considered a 'brand', then the band has left quite a long-lasting impact on my work. The images and themes Jarvis Cocker created in collaboration with the likes of Peter Saville and Nick Knight for the *A Different Class*, *This is Hardcore* and *We Love Life* albums and music videos were a large influence for me early on, and still tend to come up in my work and inspiration mood boards from time to time."

Art and design for FM4 Radio by Typejockeys, Vienna.

"The explosion of youth culture has given Singapore a breath of fresh air. They are challenging conventions, experimenting with new styles, mixing and matching influences from around the world. It's a blend of old and new, East and West, wacky and formal. Gone are the days when you needed to grow up to be a doctor or engineer; the youth no longer feel the need to live up to expectations…and art is more respectable now than ever. Encouraging creativity and innovation is one way to stand out from competitors, and Singapore is a very competitive country. Smart businesspeople know that creativity and innovation are long-term strategies if they plan to be in the market for a long while. The bottom line is still results. It is what they are always looking for."

52

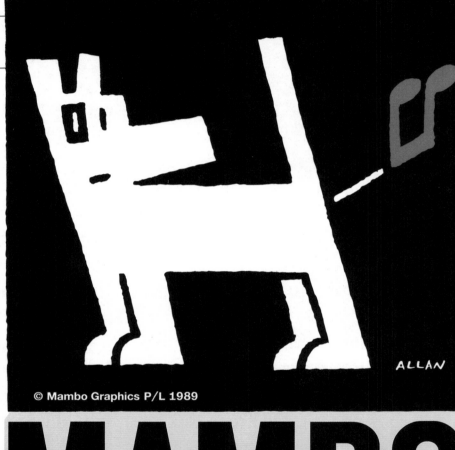

© Mambo Graphics P/L 1989

The fact that Australia is on the other side of the world from the US and Europe makes a difference to the creative culture there, both negative and positive. The negative is that the youth must feel very far away from the American and European culture that they're connected to, but the positive is that this makes them highly self-sufficient. They have their own twist, which is something I'm always excited to see. "Local is Lekker" is how they describe it in South Africa, and Australian creativity is definitely lekker.

I spent a bit of time in Sydney, where I met up with some great agencies and creatives. I also got down with the youth to find out what made them tick (and buy).

"In the context of youth advertising, my hero is anyone who doesn't resort to using an image of a DJ. That'll appeal to the youth!"

"I think location should make more difference than it tends to. There is a world of ad-land out there that usually resides on the pages of *Luerzer's Archive* or similar magazines dedicated to the visual pun and the small logo. This type of work connects with no one but the industry itself. Real work that aims to connect with real local people should, by definition of where they live and how they behave, feel very different depending on where you are in the world. Sure, there are themes that are common. But I think the more local the work, the more interesting it tends to be."

52   198   **Down Under –**   ↓ **James Brown**
               Aussie creativity   ↓ **Jonathan Kneebone**

"My favourite youth brand has to be Benetton – white baby in black hands, black baby in white hands – simple and to the point and a good message. Also WWF, Sea Shepherd, Mash! Because they all have a soul."

"The Glue Society sets out to bring the spirit of the brand to life. The original owner of 42 Below told us, 'There's no good reason why we started making vodka in New Zealand.' He said to people, 'Let's do it – because we can.' The act of turning something mundane (water) into something special (vodka) for no other reason than because you can felt like a very inspiring start point. We therefore decided to use unbranded artists (basically us in white suits) to turn mundane things into art, and use films of the proceedings to spread the word. For us, this is the definition of communication art: when a brand expresses its personality by doing something."

"What's different Down Under? Advertising, peer pressure/acceptance, a healthy Australian dollar, a unique product with an interesting brand-culture and a rich, absentee parent. While Mambo falls directly into the 'product/culture' category, we are not averse to accepting the occasional patronage of a rich, guilt-ridden parent. We stay fresh by remaining heavily involved with the people we clothe and by not ignoring our own proven instincts. And patience. Knowing that someone here will eventually come up with a good idea (as long as we don't leave them locked in the toilet for too long). Mambo is a brand that is driven by instinct and passion… and a very creative crew. Over the years we have been able to surround ourselves with a wildly talented group of artists and friends who are never short of a good idea."

SNEAKERPEDIA

An online, ever-evolving encyclopedia for sneaker-heads – what's not to like?

Sneakers logged.

"It came about because we had a brand called Foot Locker that is hugely challenged by the likes of Nike, Adidas and others, who have many more marketing dollars. However, when you look at it, Nike has Nike and Adidas has Adidas – but there are many people out there who share a passion for all sneaker brands. The main brands can't share that, as they are their own manufacturers, but Foot Locker can. There was a great opportunity – we couldn't keep up with what they spend in broadcast or social or Facebook promotions, but we could go out and build a connection to anyone who loves sneakers and get that reflecting back on Foot Locker, because the essence of the brand is 'enthusiasm beyond reason'. We can share it with anyone who has this enthusiasm for sneakers. And sharing rather than saying works – if we say it, people might not believe it, but if we share it then it's so much more powerful."

54 **The power of rebellion**

Nothing is more powerful than rebellion, but it is a slippery slope to climb, as you need to prove that your idea is about rebellion and not rebellion-lite. The actual idea and spirit of rebellion is a force that sells units more than pretty much anything else, and that is a fact. A good or big idea that includes rebellion will almost certainly get you the publicity and coverage that your brand demands, but it's what you do or where you go once you've got the attention that will make a difference.

In these days of economic worries, it could be said that brands often attempt to roll out rebellion-lite. Take Benetton's 'UNHATE' campaign at the end of 2011. At first it appeared that the Italian brand had – with a nod to our friend Oliviero – stepped up to create something that got people talking about Benetton once again. But then a few days after the launch of the campaign, Benetton caved in to pressure from the Vatican, which had complained about the poster of the Pope kissing the Sheikh of the Al-Azhar Mosque.

This, in my opinion, is precisely the reaction you want when uniting brands + rebellion. However, the apology signalled a growing fear in the creative world, where agencies and brands are so scared of losing money (and clients) that they will not take risks. Or they will only pretend to take risks. When things like this happen it looks like the bean-counters have taken over the creative. Following the riots in the UK in the summer of

"I recognize the unconscious spirit of rebellious independence that exists in all of us, and the compulsions you or I may have to demonstrate that we wear no man's yoke."

"The Dr Pepper 'What's the worst that could happen' campaign got pulled because it went too far. It included a takeover of your Facebook status, and the riskier it was, the more points you got to increase your chances of winning £1,000 or something like that. For some reason one of the lines used was '2 girls 1 cup' (a really nasty online video that no one should ever watch) and a 15-year-old's mother Googled her daughter's Facebook status, which happened to be the video of '2 girls 1 cup'. And the agency lost the client. Then there is the Burger King 'Whopper Sacrifice' (delete ten friends and get a free Whopper) that Facebook banned, but it still got them loads of publicity – it's an example of pushing it too far, but in a good way."

The 24/7 excuse for everything

Ron English doesn't hold back.

54   **The power of rebellion**

From a killer series of Adshel takeovers by Eyesaw.

2011, brands and the advertising industry need to ask why these inner-city kids had been sold aspirations that they couldn't afford, and were willing to risk prison to go out and steal. The industry needs to look after and nurture the talent and spirit of the youth – not just the stuff they are selling. This energy and vibrancy are what could make future advertising great, and it all comes from the power of rebellion.

The rebel sell is a powerful force to harness to your brand. I was always a rebel. I got kicked out of art school several times and fired from agencies around the world, but always redeemed myself by pulling out a decent piece of work – until I really went too far – so I know about using the power

of rebellion. It is so important to remember that rebellion is the bottom line, the energy needed, for a lot of successful youth advertising. I'm not talking about overthrowing governments here; more about fighting against what you're supposed to do, what you're told to do, or what you don't want to be doing. It's such an easy thing to say, but it's hard to show. Rebellion – it's an attitude, a look, a feeling, and yet it's something that can't be bottled. Back to that again! Bill Hicks is a great example. So is Amelia Earhart. So is Fela Kuti.

And the obvious thing is not always what works. In the old way of "ad-thought" the brands would want to use Biggie or 2Pac to attract the youth, but this is exactly how not to think. You have to

54   205   The power of rebellion

↓ Federico Lombardi. Vatican spokesman
↓ Jordan Sharon & Keith Hamm.
Directors, Cousins

"[Benetton] shows a grave lack of respect for the pope, an offence to the feelings of believers, a clear demonstration of how publicity can violate the basic rules of respect for people by attracting attention with provocation."

"If *Mad Men* has taught us anything about modern advertising, it's that it is important for advertising ITSELF to be truly rebellious, rather than some Kabuki theatre of rebellion. Some mainstream brands will not survive this digital transition because they will be out-niched by their competitors who recognize, and truly understand, their youth market. These brands will create innovative, challenging content even if they have to do it under the guise of an unsanctioned campaign."

look beyond the old model. Rebellion is something
that is hard to harness, but it is so effective if you
can pull it off.

"If the youth are not initiated into the village,
they will burn it down just to feel its warmth."

**Co-branding ad takeover from
Ludo in Paris.**

A DELICIOUS SHORT CUT TO ATTENTION DEFICIT DISORDER
Killkidds
GETS KIDS SUPER HYPERACTIVE!
SUGAR
FROSTED FAT
A NATURAL SOURCE OF SATURATED FAT!
THEY'RE
GR-R-ROOOOSS!
FREE
RITALIN
dose included
POPAGANDA

Ron English infiltrates the cereal shelf at a store near you.

"I think there are some brands that can behave rebelliously, but it has to be relevant and appropriate. Many of our clients are rebellious in the sense that they don't follow accepted wisdom – they will do the right thing for their audience, not what everyone else does. It's about swimming against the tide of normality, being non-conformist. Innovator brands like Apple and Nike are great examples. I think the smartest brands understand that the youth have an extreme amount of good in them and, yes, they want to rebel, but mostly only against the bullshit they endure in their lives, and this includes the crap advertising they are fed day in and day out. Innovator brands get this and work towards fulfilling the aspirations of their audience, to make them fulfil their aims to be better people. A strategy that every brand should adopt is to 'make me better', and if you can't make me better, then jog on."

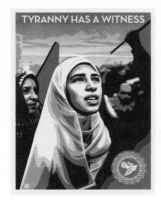

Shepard Fairey's poster for the Human Rights Watch organization.

"Advertisers are struggling to figure out how to reach young people. Many of the traditional ways of communicating don't work in the digital world and they can be invasive or annoying. No one feels this more than those who've grown up with the Internet, especially when you have experienced the Internet as a sanctuary/escape from the real world. As we see it, the challenge for advertisers moving forward is to reach these ever-increasing social niches (particularly online ones), without creating content that completely co-opts these identities or feels contrived."

Ron goes for Coke's jugular.

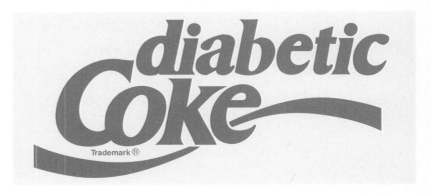

55   210   **Some renegade action**   ↓ **Eyesaw.**
Artist

"It's the constant bombardment of advertising that creeps into every aspect of our lives and the greed of the capitalist society that we are all slaves to. All I aim to do is make the viewer question their surroundings, the world we live in and their role in society. By placing my work in prime advertising space, the passer-by is almost fooled into believing my work is an advert selling more shit they don't need. As my work offers no explanation as to what is being sold, the viewer is made to ask their own questions and draw their own conclusions. As a result I gain great satisfaction knowing I have removed a crap advert from circulation and replaced it with one of my works, and just maybe opened someone's eyes to one of society's downfalls."

56

Knowledge is contagious. How you spread it is up to you. Infect 仕切り仕切り

Spreading the word by any means necessary. Serious confectionary from the Infect truth® campaign.

truth® is an innovative, highly successful youth smoking prevention campaign from the US that uses rebellion (against the giant tobacco firms and lobbyists) to get its message across. It was launched nationally in February 2000 by the American Legacy Foundation, a national public health foundation dedicated to reducing tobacco use, along with advertising partners CP+B of Miami and Arnold Worldwide of Boston. It was modelled on an earlier, highly successful campaign created in 1997 by Florida public health officials and CP+B to address the issue of youth tobacco use in the state of Florida. truth® is the only national anti-smoking campaign in the US not directed or controlled by the tobacco industry. Its success stems from the language, tone and use of media channels that connect directly to youth – a target audience for tobacco products – who need to be told the truth, hence the name.

truth® gives teens the inside scoop on all aspects of tobacco use, from the marketing and manufacturing tactics of the tobacco industry, to the health effects and the social consequences of smoking. Since the beginning, smoking has been a behaviour used by teens to display rebellion. truth® understands this and provides other ways for teens to rebel – by choosing not to smoke. This has to be their choice, and it is one that isn't going to be made from just visiting a website, or watching a "cool" film or some such piece of communication. This choice will only be

↓ **Cheryl G. Healton, DrPH, President and CEO, American Legacy Foundation**

"truth® has become an iconic part of teen popular culture by not compromising on the idea that teens appreciate being asked to make their own informed decisions and not being told what to do. Of course, the way in which truth® presents information has been and will continue to be provocative, because that is what teens most at risk of smoking respond to best."

The unsweet truth. A drive-by float rams the message home about the dangers of smoking.

made when the teens realize that a true rebel is one who doesn't smoke – one who is bucking the trend.

Since the campaign's inception, research has showed that it has been successful in changing teens' behaviour and attitudes towards smoking. A study published in the April 2009 issue of the American Journal of Preventive Medicine found that truth® was responsible for keeping 450,000 teens from starting to smoke between 2000 and 2004, which were the first four years of the campaign's life. This is not only an impressive statistic, but is also a great message that creative communications can change and improve lives. Who says art has no real effect on life? truth®

has also won a vast array of advertising and communication awards, such as Webbys, Emmys and Clios, for the creativity used to promote the core messages, and has forged partnerships with brands such as MTV and Fuse.

↓ **Eric Asche, Senior VP of Marketing, American Legacy Foundation**

"While campaign funds have been in decline since 2003, we have evolved to extend the truth® message in even more efficient and cost-effective ways. Responding to an audience that is creating its own content and looking for further engagement with brands and campaigns, the truth® tour will continue to play a pivotal role in the years to come, and the truth® experience will be enhanced further through development of original content and integrations with our media partners."

57

One of the things that is becoming clear – one of the pure nuggets of information gold – is this: to create really successful advertising that connects with the youth, the brand or advertiser has to venture deep into their world and contribute something substantial. You can't dip in and simply scratch the surface. This world is usually defined as a subculture: music, fashion, clubs, x-sports, tattoos, as well as diversity/gender related areas (LGBT). Although this is easier said than done, it is a vital first step in any long-term game plan. Just how do you do this?

The advertiser or brand has to become a mirror in this world, reflecting back into the subculture, or even a spotlight shining on certain areas of it.

This integrates the brand, and gives it the opportunity to contribute to the subculture in a positive way – something that will have a real meaning or impact on the lives of the youth. This will come back in the long run in a kind of brand-karma. There is nothing more real or exciting than culture that has originated on or near the street. Street culture. I'm talking raves, skate, street art, hip hop, reggae, punk, grunge, Teds, rockers, mods, yadda yadda yo.... This street culture, subculture, now plays a huge part in connecting to the youth. So what happens when a brand jumps onto a certain talent or movement or happening? Does it kill it, or does it spread the word – albeit attached to a logo?

"The kids that are really interesting now are these 14-year-olds living on the housing schemes, which is obviously way out of my world, but I just know these little fuckers are having a great time and doing some wonderful things…"

"Now more than ever, your 'youth' (or otherwise) is defined by your choices, not your age. I suspect that's the reason we're continually inventing whole new categories for human beings: Tweens, Extended Youth, Generation Y, and so on. From one perspective, I'm a youth as much as any 16-year-old on a scooter."

Late-night New Delhi youth:
"Do I look funny or something?"

One question that has been lurking around my mind is: do real subcultures exist any more? I know that there are definite movements of youth which could be easily defined as subcultures. But has the digital revolution connected the youth everywhere in such a way that it is now one big movement?

When I was a teenager I could often identify the nationality of girls visiting London by the shoes they wore. French girls had high-top Adidas boots with three-colour stripes, the Italians had (more often than not) Travel Fox and the Americans wore Nike. This was before street culture had become the norm, and way before the Internet could spread the word as quick as you could type. Back then, everything was passed through magazines or word of mouth, and this was what made these tribes interesting: their differences.

As I've mentioned, culture and consumption have become tangled. I was recently part of a festival in Johannesburg, where what promised to be a bit of authentic street culture turned out to be a hastily erected shopping mall with a stage tacked onto the front. People were streaming in, buying sneakers and T-shirts, a few had them customized, and they all thought they were contributing or part of this culture, when really they were just buying stuff. This is where it goes wrong. Culture is there to be contributed to, and participated in, not

"First and foremost, unlike the United States, Europe is not a melting pot. It is probably easier to unite European teenagers around American pop cultural phenomena than around European dittos. Therefore, it is almost as difficult to become a European 'phenomenon' as it is to be a global 'phenomenon'. This is why you need creatives from each market and tailor-made strategies for how the creative should be implemented. How European youths differ from the rest of the world is very hard to tell, but generally I would suggest that education, social standing and subcultural belonging sometimes are more significant than geographical and cultural belonging."

consumed – and this is something brands can help with. A brand with vision can enable the consumer to become a contributor, rather than the other way round, which is the norm today. It is the duty of the advertiser to inspire sustainability and preservation of culture, not just sales and spin. It is a new brand of consumption, based around social capital, ecological capital and cultural capital.

"Everyone reads the same magazines, plays the same games, watches the same movies and wears the same multi-brands. The pop culture platform is pretty consistent across borders – youths are grouped as tribes rather than by nationality. One big difference is education in consumerism. For example, I believe that Sweden and Germany have the most critical consumers in the world. And that affects how you have to communicate. Consumers see through every attempt to deceive them."

"If we fast-forward not too far, a handful of years, I don't think you'll be able to separate the two: anything that's good commerce will be born of an understanding of culture, and anything that's good for a brand's cultural connection will come out of commerce. And we see this with social commerce and everything that's coming into force right now. There is no point in approaching it from a purely commercial perspective, because it all goes back to understanding people; the

American skinhead, 2010. By Adam Krause.

nuances and peculiarities around people and culture are much more rich than just a business model. Often these theories are validated by some facts, but it's not particularly demonstrative coming at this topic from an analyst's point of view. An s-commerce example of this is that huge global brands, such as P&G, are now selling millions of dollars' worth of products through Facebook. This proves the point that if a brand is in the place where people are and becomes part of the conversation, then it becomes commerce a lot easier than if it's forced on people. If you don't involve the audience then brands just try to promote their way into their worlds."

An original Scottish youth, 2010. By Martin Barker.

58 ²¹⁹

A showcase of youth and their sub/cultures from around the world: Russia, Israel, Iran, South Africa, China, Brazil, Pakistan, UK, US, Spain, Zimbabwe, Australia.

"We did what we had to do and that is why we didn't survive. Only the fakes survive. All I want is for future generations to just go, 'Fuck it, had enough, here's the truth!'"

"Where time is questioned, space remains unoccupied, neutral you'll stand, capable of infinite capability. Confused by the eye, redirected by the intellect, drove by the feet, made it by the hands #completion."

"Even though I had an exam in the morning, and we had to drive for five hours, I went to see the Chemical Brothers play. I didn't know who they were but my friend had two tickets and I never miss the opportunity to have a new experience!"

English youth captured by Samuel Munyeza.

"I feel good about the brands that are related to my interests, for example, I'm a b-boy, I do parkour as well, and I'm a pro graffiti writer. So brands have a lot of variety, I mean I can't create a shoe or sew baggy jeans at home so it feels really good when I see a shoe, shirt or markers for drawing that match my interest and make my work easy. But the problem is that these brands raise their prices week after week, which is very disappointing. There should be dialogue between big brands and youth about what we want and what these brands can do to satisfy our needs. How many students are there who can buy a $150 Nike Air Force shoe? As I live in Pakistan, $150 means around 13,000 rupees in my country. And not just shoes or clothing brands, I see the rates of everything growing on a monthly basis and youngsters like me have to settle for less because the prices are getting out of our hands. When these brands make something CATCHY, that catchy stuff should be AFFORDABLE as well, and shouldn't be made for the rich people only."

Iranian youth. By Karan Reshad.

"Advertising in Iran is like many other places in developing countries, but as long as I've known we've had a political ideology here to buy Iranian products (mostly in home equipment). But the rich buy and like Western goods. So uptown you see ads like Adidas, Givenchy, Bulgari and BMW. Downtown you see ads for some Iranian-made stuff and many, many religious ads and propaganda. I hate ads and would like to replace them with art, but, of course, advertising has an impact on urban creatures like us, to adjust our needs and our shopping plan. I try to buy what I need, and try to find the best for me by asking people or trying on my own. In other cases many of the things in advertisements are not for me (personally), I do not use a car. I like the Adidas adverts I see abroad. So advertising does have an impact, as before I hated any brand shoes, but that changed my mind. I like Mac because of the advertising and people's advice (which is also a kind of advertising). The aim of youth

A moment in east London nightlife grabbed by DJ Todd Hart.

advertising here is to promote religion more than youth culture, and they try to place importance on family and religion rather than individuality. Youth culture here is ignored."

"Youth advertising makes a huge impact on social trends and what products or brands of clothing are in fashion at a particular time. Brands have almost brainwashed young people to the point where there doesn't seem to be any originality in choice of clothing or products. Brands such as Converse and BlackBerry have become a young person's basic possessions. Everyone has at least one of the two. If you look back just five years ago, BlackBerrys were used mainly by business, personal or PR gurus, now one in five secondary school kids have one. This change in what's socially acceptable has a lot to do with how brands have changed their advertising, and also how young people are paying more attention to what music artists are wearing. What personally

French youth.
By Marylin Cayrac.

Dasha Yastrebova distils the moment perfectly. The youth by the youth, Russia.

makes me buy a product is how unique the product is, the price of the product being that it's not a bank-breaker, and if the product stands out from the crowd. I love brands such as Vans, Nike, etnies, Famous Stars and Straps, Zoo York; hate brands like Gucci, Prada, Yves Saint Laurent, Ralph Lauren – I hate them because they're made to show how much dough you have in your pocket, there's no substance or anything WOW about them, whereas the brands I like are the ones made famous by subcultures, such as skaters and emos, they express individuality way better than some overpriced Gucci bag."

Shanghai skater.

São Paulo downhill skater.

"I think the core of it is wanting to fit in, hey.
That's da main reason.., i buy my clothes so dat i
luk cool and im in dat group, i use a sony and nt a
nokia coz i wana b in da group of people who dnt
gv a damn…mst people wil say they buy sumdng
coz they love it, nt coz people love it. thats a
group of people who dnt gv a damn, so they in
dat group…we buy to fit in. Its gng to da bling, b4
streetculture use to b bout just dat, the streets…
now people who are hustlng in da streets cnt
relate, coz its bout da expensive shoes, the model
lyk grls, the flashy crib…look at str.crd, we were
at a dodgy place yet at a posh hotel…those are da
new streets. they paved wit platinum."

Kris. By Guy Pitchon.

Tel Aviv Dreek girl. By Guy Pitchon.

Sanele Gele Patrick, holding it down for Durban.

'I don't like when brands spend too much money on advertising campaigns. I'd prefer they donate it to charities :). A good example is Zara, who have no ads or commercials at all, they have a completely different production and promotion model. They opt to spend more money on placing their retail stores on high streets and in well-known places, where people will wander into their boutiques regardless of advertising. I think youth advertising is evil. It can turn children without stable views and beliefs into media zombies, and we can already see teenagers craving styles and images popularized by mass media. I don't drink Coke or Pepsi or anything of the sort, I prefer ice water, fresh juices or home-brewed drinks. The same with food. Perhaps I sound like a babushka but I love living healthy, and I'd recommend the same. The problem is, the current paradigm among youngsters is that everything reasonable, safe and healthy is 'uncool', and a lot of youth ads use that paradigm."

59

There is always something surprising coming out
of Israel, and these advertising images created by
artist Pilpeled for his extremely cult T-shirt brand
are something that stopped me in my tracks. Literally.

**Welcome to the night dream.
Dark sells.**

"The idea was to work in collaboration with
photographer Guy Pitchon, to present the
T-shirts with kids, regular kids, not models,
not cool, not hipsters, without having to resort
to using tits and sexy legs. We made them special
by using the night and animals surrounding
them – like secret friends in the dark."

60

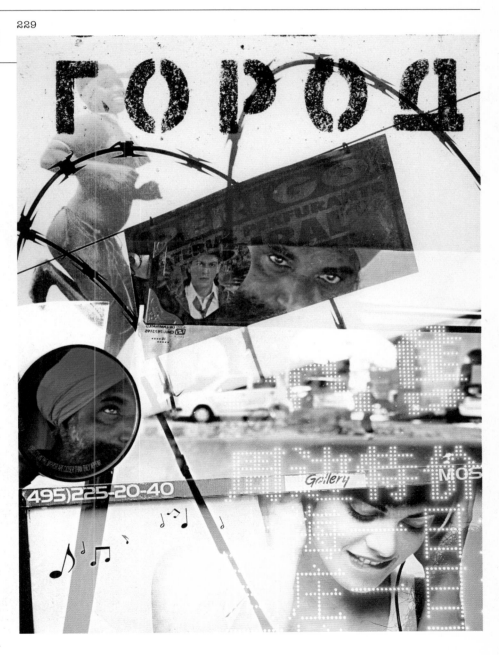

The major "emerging" (in reality most are doing better than the West right now!) markets are grouped under the BRICS banner – Brazil, Russia, India, China and South Africa – and this is where I travelled to see if I could grab a moment of clarity and capture some of the great work (and true spirit of youth) that is happening there. It is vitally important to realize that the youth in these territories have started to look inwards, instead of looking dreamily at what is coming out of the US and Europe. They have begun to understand the importance of their own cultures, their own twists on the "glocal" style, and are now proud to be different (perhaps this is the influence of Apple Inc.?).

I travelled from Moscow to Cape Town to Jo'burg to São Paulo to Shanghai to New Dehli (and Gurgaon), and loaded up my smartphone with Nike True City as well as other data on the Google Maps app, marking the places I had to check, eat, or go for meetings. This is when I appreciated how far technology has taken us. It wasn't about going to expensive restaurants and uptown bars with advertising types – no, I stayed at hostels to get closer to my subjects, and went to as many different places as possible where the youth would be hanging out in their natural habitat: skate parks, malls, clubs, festivals, fast-food joints, grungy boutiques, squares, parks, high streets, gigs, comedy clubs, etc.

The "emerging" (BRICS) markets

Advertising seeping into the back of an auto-rickshaw, India.

61

The first thing I noticed when I landed in São Paulo was that all forms of public advertising have been banned. The streets are full of street art (always a good sign) and the odd fly poster for a band or skate contest, but apart from that, there was not an advert in sight, which gave the city an almost retro feel. I also noticed that I could be in a bar or public place, full of people who looked either African, Asian, European or South American, and yet they were all Brazilian, all getting on like a house on fire, and all on the same level – unlike in South Africa, where colour still separates. I took my lunches in the local <u>lanchonetes</u> alongside the workers and ate my rice, beans and whatever meat came under the heading "simple menu", and no one batted an eyelid – I could have been one of them. Some old clichés still abound: Brazilian youth's love of heavy metal; it can be very hectic in parts of town; the fear of kidnapping is real, as attested by my friend's bullet-proof Range Rover; and the people are beautiful and completely open, something that comes into play when trying to sell to them, which will be discussed later.

If you want to know about Brazilian youth, take a walk down Rua Augusta on a Friday or Saturday night. The pavement is packed with kids of all ages, drinking at bars that are illegal but tolerated by the police. The further you walk, the more real it gets, and if you walk downtown to the end of the road you will end up in "Crack City", which is like stepping into a zombie movie.

61

Brazil – São Paulo   ↓ **Paola Colombo**
Group Director R/GA São Paulo

"Talking specifically about the Internet and communications, Brazilians are really social, and it's always been this way. They are used to being around a lot of people, all the time – they live with their family until they get married, sometimes even after they get married. The social part is integral to the culture, so when you're talking about marketing you can't forget that, especially now that social media is a part of marketing. Companies and brands want to get the word of mouth that is going to happen here, and it will happen very quickly in Brazil, since people are chattier in the way they behave. I think a lot of credibility comes from when you talk the talk online and then walk the walk outside your formal communications. Take the Nike+ platform as an example – they talk about sneakers and performance and then they let people track their data and share and challenge other people. That type of mentality is starting to come up here in Brazil; brands are starting to understand that

"The police are strange here," my friend Flip – who is São Paulo-born and bred – tells me, which is his way of saying they are totally corrupt, as we walk past a bar that openly sells cocaine. There is a strong police presence around the city. One morning I was walking along a street in an uptown area when two young guys with gold teeth and Nike tracksuits came into view walking towards me. The vibe in São Paulo is rather heavy, so I was keeping my eyes and ears open, when a van screeched to a stop behind me. Looking at the two guys in front and knowing a bit about kidnapping, I turned to check my back and saw a gun and a very tall black policeman rushing past me. The next thing I knew the two guys in tracksuits were on the ground with an assortment of firearms pointing at them. I walked on, looking back to see what was occurring. Nothing much. The police drove off, and the two guys got up, dusted themselves down, and continued walking. Just another stop-and-search on the heavy streets of São Paulo.

"I can find myself in a part of the city I've never been in before," Flip tells me as we walk away from the madness. This is something I had never even thought about: living in a city that you will never be able to know everything about. It blew my mind. After climbing a hill (the city is full of them), I looked north (downtown) and then south (uptown) and all I could see were skyscrapers, tower blocks and then some. The view was repeated for as far as I could see.

anything they throw on the web or TV will end up in social media and people will talk non-stop. Talk spreads like wildfire in Brazil. Much quicker than I've seen elsewhere."

"The Brazilian youth are open to experimenting, and not just with technology. It's the Brazilian character – you are here and we are open to you, to the new. We don't have any barriers that make us want you to prove anything to us, like for instance you will find in the US. We adapt easily. Our youth or our elders are open to almost everything. We don't have to trespass or sneak around – the Brazilians like advertising and, more importantly, like to talk about advertising. There are many different kinds of youth and I think the difficulty is in finding the right tune to talk to all of them. But be open and honest – this works always. No one here has a problem with being sold to. I think it's becoming very, very complicated in the UK and the US, where

My hostel threw a pool party on a night before a bank holiday, and it was full of youth, all having a great time and getting down to a local band, who looked and sounded like Brazilians by way of east London – so the global culture has started to make an impact. There was no major binge drinking, no obvious drug-taking. Some people were smoking weed, but that was it. At the height of the party a few people jumped in the pool, and this was when the only damage happened – they had cellphones and digital cameras in their pockets.

One of the problems with advertising here is that the budgets are not moving from TV to social media. The youth are into social media but the brands aren't following – yet. The consumers are unafraid of experimenting and trying new things, but Brazilian brands are still traditional. The marketing industry is very much structured like in the <u>Mad Men</u> days. In Brazil the average social media budget in 2012 was still only 6 per cent of the total advertising spend, compared to over 50 per cent in the US and Europe.

there is this pretence that it's not advertising. That the brands are not selling. I think people will feel really cheated when they realize what is going on. I believe in doing things openly; I think it's a mark of respect for the consumer when brands believe in what they are selling and they try to convince you of that. It's the best way for a long, honest relationship."

"I think there is a curiosity in the way people use social media or technology here. The reasons to adopt new things go way beyond the function: 'Let me see what I can do with this.' I remember when Facebook started to become popular in Brazil, people would try all the crappy games and apps. Nobody really knew why they were using Facebook, but they were using it. I think this is the way other platforms like Orkut and Twitter grew in Brazil as well."

62

This is content, consumption and culture pumping out in perfect harmony. For the launch of the centenary kit for Sport Club Corinthians Paulista, one of the most popular Brazilian soccer teams, F/Nazca Saatchi & Saatchi in São Paulo went one step further than the rest – they created a country.

"Corinthians was turning one hundred and Nike launched a country on the back of it. The ex-President Luiz da Silva was a fan, and they had him on TV collecting his passport, and because he was genuinely a Corinthian fan and the whole of Brazil knew that, it worked. Super-smart marketing from Nike. The 'embassies' were these huge pantechnicons that parked outside the stadiums and the public went and bought the one-hundred-year kits; you got a passport and it was stamped, and Nike made a fortune. So they created this sense of community and country, and set up the embassies so that if you were a member of another football team and you wanted clothing you could 'emigrate'. When I see ideas like that it doesn't make me run out and buy something Nike, but I do go, 'Damn! I wish I'd done that!'"

63

Big brands taking risks and being down with experimentation is what is needed to keep the industry fresh, especially for youth. TIM is Brazil's leading cellphone network provider. It was the first to have coverage in all of the country's states, and has over 55 million customers, so when I heard about what they were doing with R/GA São Paulo, I was immediately interested.

"Because we in Brazil are about four years behind the digital wave, the new kind of advertising taking over is not yet a reality here. But we see progress when companies start taking digital seriously. We have a client, TIM, who does a lot of traditional marketing, but also created a pilot programme for youth to experiment with crowd-sourcing, building a plan based on direct input from the users. The work we are doing with them is very much about integrating users' social lives into the programme itself and building a game around it. This yields results, and we can build a relationship with youth a lot quicker this way than with traditional advertising. These kinds of results will begin to influence the other brands."

"TIM beta started as an experiment. TIM launched the pre-paid phone plan through an app on Facebook, where people played a game to win eight chips to distribute to their friends. They got

The brown box kit.

hundreds of thousands of people signed up in no time. Then TIM asked us to relaunch this project, to help transform it into a financially sustainable product while keeping the experimental feeling, which gave us the freedom to try new stuff without being afraid of getting it wrong. If you talk to youth this way, not being afraid to fail, then it can work. Research can help to confirm the info you have already openly sourced on the social networks right from the start of the project. User-generated content often gives you the most powerful insights. People will naturally find ways to share good content, and adding a 'share' button will make it easier. They talk about things that are interesting to them, and online the word moves faster, especially through social media. The brands that take advantage of word of mouth are the ones that are fast enough to react when something picks up. You can't plan for everything, so you have to be super-fast to make something work for your brand as it goes."

"The brown box was a kit we sent to nine 'beta testers', a small group of customers that TIM used to validate ideas and prices, and gauge reactions prior to relaunching the plan. We sent them a T-shirt, a leaflet explaining the new branding and tone of the product, and a Lomo camera and films so they could continue to take part in helping TIM build the plan – they would use one of the rolls of film to take pictures of themselves, which we could then use in the new campaign.

The first set of creative materials launched online and on the website used only pictures of these guys, to reinforce the idea that it is a plan 'created by them and for them'. With the first phase of the relaunch, people who already were part of the pilot test could join and get two extra SMS chips to invite people in their network to join. One of the benefits of TIM beta is that you have unlimited calls for people within the network,

so right away they get two chips they can send to two close friends or people they would call a lot. People who were not on the pilot can use the app, which scans their social networks, to find those who belong to the programme, and ask them for chips. Those participants are notified and have the option to give their extra chips to these people or anyone else they are connected with on Facebook, Twitter or Orkut.

TIM beta has had a strong following since the pilot days, so there are quite a few communities created online to promote it. Besides these 'organic' communities, TIM also supports an official community on Facebook and Orkut, and promotes it via its @TIMTIMporTIMTIM Twitter. Current clients, once they had re-registered, could boast via the app that they had gotten the new plan. In December we also created an event for the betas (those in the network) to vote and participate in a concert that was broadcast on TV.

This also helped promote TIM beta as a product tailored for this generation, which lets them choose the benefits, bands and parts of the plan that are important to them. Again, the idea is that it is a plan 'created by them and for them'."

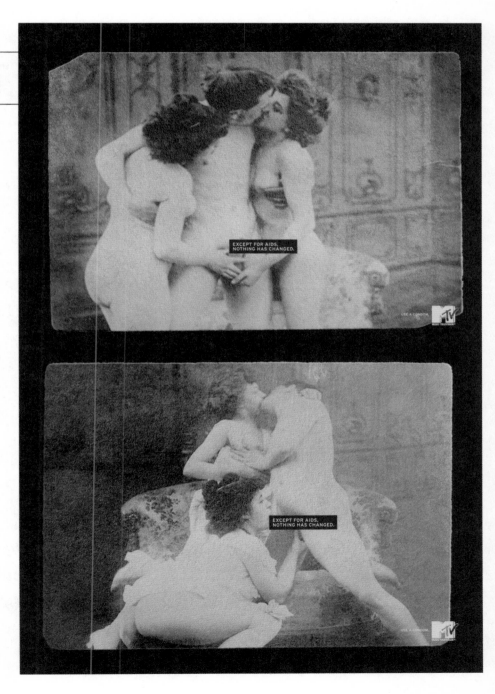

Some of the best ads I've seen in a long time are coming out of an ad agency in São Paulo called Loducca. Quite possibly the most creative and certainly the most awarded agency in South America, Loducca is a shining example of the new breed of creative agency that continually produces thought-provoking work which expands the boundaries of advertising. They have created some amazing campaigns for the likes of MTV, Red Bull, Nextel, Peugeot. A visit to their awards room tells you how far they've travelled down the creative road, and how respected they are around the world. I spent a few days hanging out with their creative director, Guga Ketzer.

What sells to youth?

"The best way to connect to the youth is not to talk about selling, but to talk about culture, behaviour, being a part of a group, because most of the times when you say, 'Buy this,' it won't work. The kids want to be a part of something; they want to create. Most of the brands are trying to tell them to do this or do that, this is cool, that is cool, but I think to connect to young people you need to put work out there that is related to something important in their lives, and then they will relate to the brand and maybe start to buy.

I believe that the guy who has a lot of friends really doesn't have any at all, and you should remember this when you try to work with the youth, because if a brand tries to talk to all of the young, they're not going to engage with anyone. So you gotta understand who are your kids, and then try to create something. Kids have a lot

of information right now and they have a short attention span, so if you don't create something that makes them stop for a second and go, 'Whoa, what the fuck!' then you will not even begin to relate to them. You need to talk to their hearts and minds in a different way. We all used to be kids and we all wanted to be rebels and change the world, whatever it was – skating, graffiti, surf…and we all know that a lot of people have come before, but when you're a kid you think you're unique, you're the first. This is the spirit you need to keep alive in advertising. This is what is important: not to sell, not to talk about money. You have to remember what it was like if you want to create work that connects to them, to be as crazy as a kid. Like, 'Why not?' Go to the edge.

Of course, at the end of the day this is a business, but kids don't need to know about the business, they want to be connected to the cool shit, and brands need to support the youth's behaviour.

They need to go with the flow and allow their own personality to seep slowly into the kids' lives. Tons of brands are trying to connect with artists, bands – all those guys who represent something for the kids. This is one way forward."

What is different about the Brazilian youth?

"Visually, everyone looks the same. The skin may be lighter, but the way kids dress is almost the same. However, in Brazil we have this thing – we love life. We go to the beach, we have fun, we don't have many issues with sexuality, and this all rolls over into a very laid-back way of life. Not lazy, just different. Economically speaking, Brazil is now huge. The kids are globally well connected, but they behave differently. No binge drinking, no real drug problems. They drink or take drugs to have fun, not to forget their problems or have a fight. They look the same as the kids from other parts of the world, but they

TO LAUNCH MTV'S NEW CONCEPT,
WE USED ONE OF MUSIC'S UNIVERSAL SYMBOLS.

**2 BAND T-SHIRTS BECOME
1 NEW MTV T-SHIRT.**

2011

behave differently. Most teens around the world hate their parents, and in Brazil they hate their parents too, but they will go to the beach, enjoy themselves. Kids in Brazil are not so depressed. We don't have a unique tribe right now – we have hipsters, grunge, heavy metals, emo guys, and the slums and favelas, and, of course, there are kids who are obsessed with fame, money and expensive cars. This is global. We are obsessed with soccer stars, the same as in the UK."

What is your "fuck me!" brand moment?

"Mine was discovering MTV. In the 1990s we had no Internet, and when I first saw some videos on MTV I was like, 'Oh my god!' And then the promo clips with the MTV logo – they were insane, and were made with huge artists at the time. It was so good because when I was a kid I loved to surf and skate, and I loved brands like Powell-Peralta, Steve Caballero and Mark Richards, but visually

I was affected by MTV. We had a Brazilian MTV on cable with American clips, but the VJs were all cool Brazilians and knew exactly how to communicate with us. It was a revolution. All our homegrown artists were on MTV with their clips. It was a true connection. And when I started working with MTV it was genius. I worked with them for twelve years before going to Loducca."

How do you stay up in the game?

"I'm hungry for everything. I've not become fat and complacent; I'm hungry all the time, as I realize that I don't really know anything. I need always to be creating stuff, and ultimately my job is about learning to understand people. I have to have this sensibility about people, and be curious about what makes them behave in certain ways in certain environments. I want to create good things. Like Steve Jobs says, 'Stay hungry, stay foolish,' and I think this is a great

MTV "Balloons" video, zooming towards Cannes.

philosophy, because otherwise we have this habit of taking ourselves way too seriously. The most foolish thing can be the most creative, the most brilliant. Like the guy from Droga5 having the idea to tag Air Force One. That's fucking genius. The best ideas are always around. Like when we said, 'Why don't we do an ad that's edible…' We did a magazine ad where you hit the page and an airbag inflates. No way? I'm always pursuing the 'why not?' You can't do that in an ad – why not?"

Does celebrity sell?

"We don't have tabloids in Brazil. You guys are obsessed with celebrity. We have celebrity magazines that sell, but not that well. Because we have sex all around us, we're not like, wow! Like with P-Middy – no one cared in Brazil. If you go to a beach in Rio you'll see some real asses. Kids in Brazil are fine with our sexuality and we just wanna have fun. Kids just want to explore their sexuality, and this means we're not obsessed when we see an outline of an ass. It's no big deal."

65

South Africa has one of the most exciting, culturally diverse and rapidly expanding youth markets in the world. It's the jewel in Africa's crown where the teens outnumber the oldies by two to one, which means that there is an immense possibility for a vast market, if handled correctly. Alongside Brazil, this is where the future of youth advertising will come from, and this is where I would set up an agency if I was going to pick a location.

Before the end of apartheid, the dominant imagery used in South African advertising was "Beer, Boks, and Braai" (Springboks – rugby; Braai – a bit like a BBQ but a lot tastier), and this was all pretty much derived from Afrikaans culture. The birth of the Rainbow Nation heralded a massive cultural shift,

and with this came a whole new set of influences. It was during this time that I worked as an art/creative director in Cape Town, just as the country was beginning to come alive with creativity, and it is out of this freedom that some of the most creative work in the world has been born in the last few years.

I travelled to Cape Town (iKapa) and Johannesburg (eGoli) to see just how much the advertising industry had developed, and in the short space of time I'd been away, a serious number of agencies had started producing world-class work. I also spent some time with the youth, from Cape Town, Port Elizabeth, Soweto and Durban, who now make up a vital part of the market. One common denominator is that they all love their

---

65

252　　**South Africa**

↓　**Mthandeni Msomi. Durban youth blogger**
↓　**Wireless G. Social activist/cultural curator**
↓　**Pete Case. Executive Creative Director, Gloo**

"How can I blog about R900 shoes, when I can't even afford airtime?"

"In South Africa, the future of youth advertising is guerrilla marketing, concepts, collaborations, blogging and partying!"

"The youth market is increasingly blanking out the direct advertising messages from brands. Whether ignoring or skipping ad breaks on TV, binning branded SMSs, or simply paging past ads in magazines, they rely more on social connections and peer commentary to make and influence their purchase decisions. These social connections are typically a mixture of online sources from blogs, sites and opt-in information streams, mixed with real-world connections with friends and the social groups they belong to. More often than not, the information that grabs their attention is connected to someone they trust, as opposed to a commercial brand

BlackBerry Messenger, and their sneaker brands. Unfortunately, there is still a colour barrier separating young people from one another, but I was lucky to be part of a street culture festival that used people's love of sneakers to travel under the colour radar and bring everyone together. It worked, and I got to witness the Rainbow Nation in full swing, with rich white Capetonians getting down with the real-deal street hustlers from Soweto and Durban. They were all brought together in a revitalized part of downtown eGoli by a German brand of sportswear. Funny old game, but it was wicked to see it working. However, on the flip side, there is 40 per cent unemployment among 18 to 25-year-old males, with little chance that they will ever find employment in their lifetime, and

what was once one of the best education systems in Africa is now one of the worst. The youth don't have access to training to give them the skills to find half-decent jobs. This shows just how important brands could be if they actively contributed to people's lives. Africa is a continent where corporate responsibility should play a massive part in the community, social and educational lives of the youth. And this is something that I want to get my hands dirty with in the future. One thing to remember is that because of the apartheid control orders (making it illegal for more than three people to get together), spreading messages by word of mouth was the only way to communicate for ANC cells. This is something that still works today through the townships. Word of mouth is still king.

broadcasting a mass message to them. As an added layer to this, the youth are increasingly interested in the way the brand is behaving beyond the product or service. With the new age of transparency created by the Net, it's easy for consumers to see behind the brand logo and into the reality of what a company is doing. Whether it's demonstrating a social conscience or an approach to the production process itself, these activities often further influence the youth's decision to purchase when comparing two similar products."

66

GOOD BOY,
NOW, ROLL BACK.

THE ONE AND ONLY
wonderbra

THE PUSH-UP PLUNGE BRA.

John Hunt is a South African advertising legend. He started the agency Hunt Lascaris in 1983 before forming TBWA\Hunt\Lascaris, and went on to create iconic Wonderbra campaigns following the strategy developed by TBWA in London. Today he is the creative director of TBWA\Worldwide.

What do you think makes youth advertising stand out?

"I think that for starters, the youth don't like being advertised at, so there's the first strange anomaly. If they see you coming from 200 metres, shouting, 'I'm cool,' they smell a rat, so I think the days of advertising at them straight on are probably gone. If you're really cool you don't have to shout about it. The moment you do, everyone knows you're not! So it's one of those strange things that you have to keep playing with in a pure advertising sense. I am an old fart but I'm lucky as I have 15-, 17-, and 23-year-old kids who keep me desperately honest in terms of this kind of thing. The youth like to discover your brand more than being told about it, and also you have to be something. We handle Apple globally in a very concentrated fashion (out of TBWA\Chiat\Day), and the products are cool or connected or whatever, and a lot of the time our job is to make sure that the advertising doesn't get in the way.

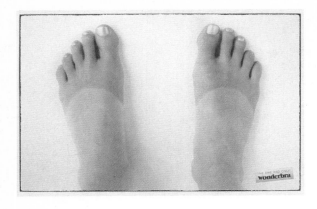

The product design, how it works, how it connects with the youth is extremely smart, and the articulation of the brand comes from what it is. Then the advertising is nothing more than a sort of 'Hey we're here!' and then you get out of the way. The youth is attracted to the brand for what it does, as opposed to what we say it is."

Youth advertising has become less about the ads and more about events, etc. – more like sponsorship of people and talents...

"If you look at the work we did with Gatorade, a 25-year-old brand with a stretched youth demographic, we were doing all the standard things to make the brand appropriate, and then we came up with this marvellous idea of 'replay'. We took an iconic American football college game that had taken place twenty years before, in which two rivals ended in a draw, and we got them to play that game again with the same team, same cheerleaders, same venue. It was a massive success. It was like distilling or bringing back

your youth. Gatorade was the sponsor of the event, which sold out in thirty seconds. The product was super-endorsed by the fact that the players were still playing a tough game of football, but twenty years on! The three months of training that the players had to go through became content, ESPN ran documentaries about how to pull back or relive your youth, and these are now in their third season. It went from football to ice hockey to basketball, and people in other sports began petitioning Gatorade to be in the next iconic game that gets replayed. It ticks every kind of box – the result is that it has become a very, very cool brand, but because of what it's doing. You read about the guy with a beer gut who is going to have to work his ass off and suck it up again as he's not going to let his team down, and the second- or third-stage info is that Gatorade has all this good stuff in it that helps you do that. In the end, of course, the brand becomes cool, but it's not the advertising agency saying it is. This is about doing something,

and the youth will then decide that because
your brand is behaving like this – as opposed to
advertising like this – it's cool. They close the last
third of the gap."

**So it's a bit like building a bridge over a chasm and the last quarter of the
bridge has to be built from the other side by the youth coming towards you.**

"Yes. They will anoint the values of whatever they
think of the brand rather than you."

Do you consider online tweeting, blogging, etc., to be word of mouth?

"To a degree it is, as it's the connective tissue,
but there is so much static, white noise, that
you have to be careful. I don't necessarily think
the job is done when you get two million people
tweeting something, because it can evaporate
just as quickly as you created it. It's the same
with Facebook going crazy, your website getting
ten million hits – it's all an indication of a thumbs
up, but be careful of the way the youth interact
with the brand. It can be very mirage-like:

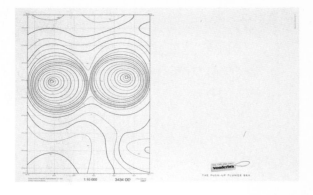

it's there and it's real, but a brand should have some values or genuine ways it connects. If you are using Twitter, etc., as a measure of success I would be a little cautious. It is a sort of word of mouth, but the question is – to what end? Are the youth saying, 'I like it,' and do they like it to such an extent that there is a propensity to buy? Our world used to be a little bit simpler…"

Does research have to be done in a new way?

"Research has its place, but it's a delicate tool that should be controlled by masterful people, because most research, in my opinion, creates its rules based on the past. We know X, and without even meaning to we forward project that, whereas in youth advertising particularly, the stuff that works normally doesn't have a precedent. That's where intuition has to come in. You have to be so careful with youth advertising in presuming that even the last three years will be relevant to the next three.

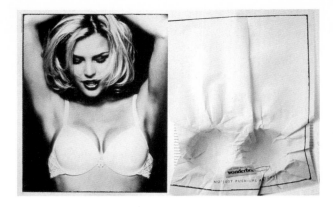

Take tablets – when they first came out everyone
dismissed them as something that wouldn't
work, mainly because there was no precedent.
Instinctively, Jon Ive – or whoever made the
call – thought that tablets were the way forward,
and he was completely right! I'm not sure how
research would have coped there, for instance.
You have to be very knowledgeable about how
kids think versus having a cupboard full of stuff
from the past that you overlay on top of what
they say to you. It's a tough one. It goes back to
your mission statement/book title about trying
to bottle the unbottle-able. Research can be very
helpful, but it's a delicate process. It's all about
how you do it."

67

"There is always the risk/reward window. We did
a lot of work for Nando's. In the early days they
wanted to launch their Peri-Peri sauce and they
needed to get it into supermarkets at a time when
no one knew the brand and the supermarket guys
were scared. We made one ad that we sent to all
the buyers and ran in magazines. It had a picture
of the bottle and the headline: 'Oral Gratification.
Isn't that what he's always been asking you for
anyway?' The buyers all fell over and bought
it by the dozen when it appeared in women's
magazines. It was high risk, but imagine if we
just talked about the ingredients of the sauce!
There's always that risk/reward quantum, and
with youth even more so – hit the bull's-eye and
they will beat a path to your door. Their response
isn't based on could, should, would; they act
viscerally: 'You got me, I'm in!'"

68

Levi's®
513
EVA
Bootylicious
and Bold
Cut to flatter and flaunt
the Booty Zone.
Sexy low front rise with
curve-friendly rear.

The Black Diamond is the term for one of the most powerful emerging demographics in South Africa. Since the end of apartheid the local and global brands have been scrambling to sew up the market and capture the money of the youth. In the beginning, agencies tried to sell an aspirational white lifestyle to the newly empowered South Africans, but this fell on its arse, as you may imagine. I experienced this when, after I had produced some of my best work for the black South African youth, I was always asked to "tone it down" and "make it less edgy"; the people making the creative decisions were white, and the market was black. It took a few years for the message to filter through that this approach wasn't working and the important thing was to recognize the youth for what they were, not what they were perceived to be: black, young, South African and proud. The term "Black Diamond" was coined by the marketing industry to describe the emerging middle classes who have a voracious appetite for global brands. There is a huge youth section of this market looking up longingly at the shelf marked "luxury". It has a powerful pull, and this is not necessarily a good thing.

On the other side of the coin come the Smarteez. Instead of aspiring to the rich, white culture of South Africa (and the West), the Smarteez are trend-setting black teens who are looking in at themselves and celebrating their own local twist

68

264

**The Black Diamond
vs Smarteez**

↓ **Roger Young.
Writer, filmmaker & journalist**
↓ **GG Alcock. CEO and founder, Minawe**

"Oblivion and sneakers separate the South African youth from their rand."

"I like to tell people that black people in South Africa do not westernize, they modernize. So as they get the trappings of a Western society – Levi's, BMWs, BlackBerrys, etc. – they appear to be what we call coconuts: black on the outside but white on the inside. Yet they are not; they retain their cultural identity and many of the values and behaviours that go with this. We read often about whiteys having an uproar in some elite suburb because their black neighbour had a sacrifice ceremony and slaughtered an ox next to the Jacuzzi. Or some millionaires insisting on *lobola* (dowry) being paid for their daughter. These stories make the headlines, but on an everyday level people in the Black Diamond sector are wealthy, Western in appearance, but strongly still Xhosa, Sotho, Zulu or whatever the case may be from a cultural perspective. In the same way

on what is happening globally. They embrace influences from overseas, as well as examining their own cultural heritage of self-sufficiency and developing their own visual language. Under apartheid, word of mouth was vital to black communities' survival. Today this network is still in effect, but it now spreads word of cultural and other issues.

One great example of how these new markets need to be taken seriously and researched properly is the story behind Levi's EVA jeans. South African agency Instant Grass was employed to see why the Levi's brand wasn't selling that well among black girls and, through their network of "grasses" (youth informers), they discovered that the local girls were not buying the jeans as they didn't fit their "bigger asses". They helped Levi's to understand that the African girls are very proud of their curves, and proud that they're shaped differently from white girls. Levi's took this on board and, together with Instant Grass and a group of young female grasses, rapidly developed the EVA jeans, exclusively for the South African market. The jeans outsold all projections and in 2011 Levi's rolled out the Curve ID brand worldwide, inspired by the success of the EVA jeans bootylicious model.

I guess a Jew in America is all things American yet holds on to and performs his Jewish culture. It is often difficult for marketers because they see black westerners, they try to market to them and fail and wonder why. So the Black Diamonds are still an elusive group."

"The Black Diamond represents the self-actualized and flash segment of the market ready to part with enormous amounts of cash for luxury brands. But, at the same time, their sense of community and roots run very deep. Supporting the family and financing proper burials for loved ones, etc., is so important that no expense is spared there."

"Clichéd assumptions that black youth are like American rap culture youth don't work. We have lots of very powerful South African fashions that are stronger and resonate better. In music, Kwaito is a huge local style. Gospel is the biggest selling music style in the youth market! The culture is

Adidas branded combi.

moving very fast. A saying I stole from someone applies very strongly to this group: when the pace of change inside your business is slower than the pace of change outside your business, your business is dead. Often advertisers catch on to new styles and cultures way after the youth have moved on, and in doing this they become so yesterday. Remember the majority of our youth speak a language of their own making: Scamto, a creole-type mix of English, Zulu, Afrikaans and a little Sotho. To keep up or be in touch is difficult unless you can speak this language and you are comfortable going into the townships and hanging in an environment that is foreign to many white and black suburban residents. Township youth are disparaging about what they call 'Model C' youth. Model C was a school category where township kids could go to former white schools in the suburbs. This resulted in a class whom many see as snobs and wannabe whiteys with unaccented English and rap styles.

Smarteez style from Soweto youth.

Township youth see them as out of touch, not really cool, yet many of the Model C people are those who get the jobs in ad agencies. I often find myself in brand offices explaining some new cultural style to a black person, which always seems absurd!"

According to scientists there are 237 reason why we have sex. Amazingly, you dont need a license to have sex, or which is a shame because we'd all be better at it if we had to pass our learners beforehand. Having sex in South Africa is like learning to drive during an F1 race - a wrong move can put you in harms way. Before you drop your Levis® jeans again (for which ever one of the 237 reasons.), heres one thing you need to know.

The first few weeks after you have become infected with HIV is the most dangerous time of your life. HIV is a clever trickster - raging wildly unchecked in your body because your antibodies at first dont recognize it as a threat. Your viral "load" skyrockets - making you the most highly infectious you will ever be to anyone of your partners. But you feel and look absolutely normal. Heres the real bitch: if you test during this period, you'll come out negative (because the test "asks" the antibodies if they have begun to fight HIV - which they haven't because they are blind to it in the first weeks). Eventually you developed some minor flu-like symptoms as your antibodies catch a wake-up that HIV has done a shock & awe on your body. They immediatley kick some HIV ass, dropping you to what seems like utter normality. During this whole HIV ride you never really feel bad so you never really think you have HIV. After your antibodies do a Chuck on the HIV, you're in the "asymptomatic" (big science word) period and it lasts years (5-10). Here you look and feel fine but you'll test HIV Positive. eventually antibodies get tired and HIV begins to take its toll - and this is when folks begin to get diagnosed with AIDS. Thanks to stigma & ignorance, too many peeps wait until they are too sick to seek medical help and that is a death sentence. But those who are proactive in managing their condition do very well. HIV is a chronic but manageable disease like diabetes, if discovered early. It does, however, absolutely suck because it means you spend the rest of your life managing a damn virus. Levis® Red for life is all about working it out for yourself. Check out for Red for life to Clothing at Levis® shops. Check out for the Red for life /new Start mobile VCT at a public location near you. Sex is beautiful. Thats why we give away beautiful Levis® branded condoms. Test yourself. Learn the truths. Make your Plan. ♥

Tapping into the style of the Smarteez: a print ad for Levi's Red for Life Aids awareness programme.

69

Since 2007, Soweto has become a focal point for the surrounding area and, perhaps, one of the most creative places in South Africa. It is a reaction to – and the polar opposite of – affluent Sandton, where most of the big agencies have always had their Jo'burg offices. Back in the day, Soweto was a destination for people looking to have a good time, and although it was a pretty dangerous place for whites during apartheid, it always attracted the open-minded and progressive. It was a very inspirational place for me back in the 1990s, as this white middle-class boy had never seen anything like it. In the last couple of years it has become a creative hub, based around a shop/collective called Thesis.

In previous years, we would have seen the inhabitants of Soweto looking out at what the white world was doing, wanting to leave and move to the "nice" areas of the city and understand white culture, but through campaigns like "I Love Soweto", and the work of Thesis Social Jam, the attitude now is less about what you are doing and more about what they are doing (as inhabitants of Soweto). The local creatives have built their own base and are proud of their yard, and because of this they don't feel the need to leave – "I love my neighbourhood, my area."

Thesis originally opened as a small concept store, where they made their own T-shirts with Soweto-inspired designs in a Smarteez style, and it grew

"Thesis Social Jam illustrates a new point of view about what Soweto is now, or at what level of thinking they should be at! It's a lifestyle brand that shows Soweto in a new light. It was born in the streets; after starting out buying second-hand clothes and reconstructing them, we launched on 27 August 2005 in a non-existent-budget fashion show on the streets. After that we went on to open the Thesis store in Mofolo, Soweto, on 16 June 2007.

The creative edge of Soweto lies in its adaptation of world happenings and interpretation of them in a way that reflects local roots and history. The people from Soweto will constantly be inspired by what is happening around them in order to show that they're a part of something bigger. The need to express oneself in a space will always push Sowetans to a place other people have not gone to. This statement rings true for subcultures like Smarteez and Thesis."

from there. It is a comfortable place with couches and initially people came just to hang out. It soon morphed into something else as they began running a once-a-month get-together called the Thesis Social Jam. In contrast to the club scene, it didn't grow from a party, but from a creative space, where everyone and anyone could share, interact and discuss how they might begin to change their community. This was a catalyst for the development of Soweto as a whole.

In a typically South African way, it has its own personality, its own style. In comparison to the Black Diamond movement, Thesis is very creatively driven; Black Diamond is more about the bling and the money, the fame and the right brands. It is like Supreme vs BMW. Thesis are global cool-kids, but they are moving all the time. The scene they are building around them is a kind of reverse integration: all the cool and white kids from the city (who might previously have been too scared to come to a township, or wouldn't have had a reason to do so) are now being lured in as they can see that something creative is happening.

Everything Thesis does is part of a collaborative process. When Public Enemy came out to South Africa, they did a show on the Saturday night, and when they got word about Thesis Social Jam the next day, they turned up and gave an impromptu performance. Collaboration and

---

69   270   **Soweto – creative hub /
Thesis Social Jam**   ↓   **Mangi Mbitshana.
Head Designer, Thesis Clothing**

"The pride that people from Soweto take in their world and neighbourhood makes people stand up and have pride in themselves. People like Mzoli's in Gugulethu take pride due to the happenings in Soweto. Sowetans make it a point that you do not need to live outside the area to know things. The mainstream influencing does not lie in physical matter, but more in sociocultural trends that are able to give growth to people and their economic aspirations. Things like Maponya Mall have changed the way people perceive Soweto and have inspired people to change what is around them."

communication are what make it such a popular place. My reaction all to this was, "Why haven't brands got Thesis Social Jam involved in selling their products?" Surely they must have a valuable insight into the mindset of the new South African consumer. These guys would be my first stop if I had a brand or product to sell to the youth of South Africa. But when I asked if the brands were queuing up, I found a situation that I've already experienced. Brands weren't that interested because nothing had been proven. They didn't trust youth with the money because they didn't have a proven track record. Brands are often keen to attach themselves to something with cultural currency, but they don't like to pay hard cash. The usual model is that they pay in swag.

69

Roses are Red
Violets are Blue
This is supposed
to rhyme

But it doesn't.

I don't expect you to care. I'm just a lonely finger with a website that's about as sad as i am. I've made movies of myself. I put them on the net. Like Paris. Only there's no Paris. And no sex. And i'm just a finger - it's not that exciting seeing me naked. So it's not like Paris at all, but you don't have to pay. You can laugh at my sadness, read what other people have said about me or send me something. Anything.

Click here to visit my world   mail me

This is a classic example of a great youth campaign, perfectly executed with an eye on the long game and a lot of patience. Pete Case, executive creative director at Gloo, tells me about how he made it happen.

What do you think makes youth advertising stand out?

"This campaign was a double winner at Cannes (silver and bronze) about five years ago (also Grand Prix at the Loeries), and is still a fave of mine. It was digitally based; the brief was to encourage a youth audience to the 5FM radio station as the general audience was over the age of 30. For the nation's youth station, this was getting too high. But we couldn't mess with the main brand image. So we created a teaser campaign around a character called Lonely Finger. The character wasn't young, old, black, white, male or female. It was essentially a finger with a sad face drawn on it and it appeared online on its own site. Very simply, we added content every few weeks: poems and sad pictures of this lonely character. Campaign elements included 'lonely' ads in the personal columns of magazines and printed cards in phone boxes, etc. The result was a huge number of conversations between us and the public who thought they were the only ones communicating with the character and trying to cheer him up. They sent in pictures and poems and all sorts of material. The campaign was a success as it tapped into the headspace of the youth at that time. The reveal was where we showed the finger walking into a bar. He meets four friends (other fingers) and becomes a hand with 'Life's better with 5' printed on it."

Why did it work?

"There was a spot of lucky timing, but also it resonated with the youth audience. It wasn't a brand wearing a cool hat and sneakers, trying to be cool. It was an unbranded communication that didn't try too hard to connect and therefore did. We let it run and we chatted on a one-on-one basis with everyone who communicated with us during the three-month campaign. It felt real and so it connected."

Visiting New Delhi and the new city of Gurgaon (where a lot of the national and international brands and agencies are now based) was a real eye-opener: these cities are the living, breathing, rapidly expanding embodiment of progress. One of my friends in India is comedian and creative director Keshavan Naidu, who spent several years abroad studying advertising in the US. He was an invaluable guide for me and a reliable font of knowledge about the youth's relationship with the Indian market. I was also fortunate to have been in India when the first media revolution took place in 1992: the launch of satellite TV. This lifted the country out of the dark ages of a single TV channel (Doordarshan) and paved the way for what would happen with the Internet. Star TV

and MTV India were piped into millions of homes. It was a strange and wonderful time. Indians were hungry for entertainment and I found myself watching bad English TV shows (The Crystal Maze) deep in the heart of the Goan jungle, or MTV in a small hill station in Tamil Nadu. These TV channels not only opened up the world of entertainment, but also provided platforms for more TV spots for the sponsors and advertisers to fill.

Despite this progress, you will still see babies tethered together at the side of a manically busy road as their mothers break and haul rocks for the men filling the holes. This is the contradiction, the duality of the place, and brings me to the first

"We need to see better online engagement in India. 'Lead India' and Sunsilk's 'Gang of Girls' were campaigns that worked well. Right now, everyone's trying to understand how best they can gather their forces online, so to speak. We have to engage with the audience here in a totally different manner. I don't think that chasing the youth online in a terribly concerted fashion is going to help brands, because unless you have a genuine story it won't matter. It all boils down to what you are saying."

"Social churn. Previous generations lived with what they got in the genetic lottery; the generation that grew up post-liberalization in 1991 had other ideas. Passivity gave way to action – migrating to larger towns and cities; taking up vocational courses to leapfrog from an agrarian life to work in the booming service sector; women joining the full-time workforce as urban migration led to the splintering of joint families and the rise

vital piece of information: there are two Indias. There is the India of the affluent, middle-class, urban dwellers; and there is Bharat, the rural, media-dark, poorer areas where the masses live, and it's these masses who will make up the majority of the youth market in the near future. The two mindsets are completely different. The real character is coming from the poorer, smaller towns and rural areas. These kids have heard of the Internet, they've heard of Facebook and they're hoping to get it, but they have never been able to afford a laptop or even a PC, though in the last year smartphones have become much cheaper. They are doing odd jobs and can buy a Chinese smartphone for next to nothing. Suddenly they've got the Internet, they are dropped in at the deep end and they're doing crazy stuff with it. Two cultures clash: their real lives and their lives online are worlds apart. We cannot imagine what this is like – Bharat life on the one hand and a global online presence on the other. And it only gets more intense when you know some of the ballpark figures. Internet penetration is around 120 million people, but the projection for smartphone Internet penetration is 600 million, and rising!

All aspects of Indian culture have been changed immensely by the digital revolution. One indicator of this is that the eunuchs, or hijras, who appear at weddings to sing, dance and give blessings, are now asking for laptops, smartphones and iPads as payment, instead of the traditional

of nuclear ones; taking risks by following the heart (my passion) instead of the head (duty to family). The quick and visible dividends that the early movers reaped had a contagion effect as their success was amplified by media and word of mouth. Be relevant to the irreverent ones. Brands like BlackBerry, which had their roots in enterprise, found new relevance with Indian youth by focusing on innovations – BBM for peer-to-peer connectivity."

"When I came back from the States after six years, things had changed drastically. The pre-liberalized India – no satellite TV, no Coke – had transformed beyond recognition. I grew up in the most interesting times to be a teenager here, because suddenly at 15 there were two hours of MTV. I was born in 1979 and grew up in the 1980s. And when MTV came, the brands followed; brands like Kellogg's appeared and tried to tell us what to eat for breakfast. We resisted, as there is a huge

cash, jewellery or saris. It says something when a subculture like this begins to chat on BBM or starts a group on Facebook.

Just as there are two sides to India, there are also two sides to the lives lead by the youth: physical and psychological. But what do the majority want to do with the new technology? How do they want to consume? While spending time with the local advertising community I discovered that, from a taste and consumption point of view, products and brands directly imported from the West do not appeal to the Indian youth. Take, for instance, McDonald's. For religious reasons they can't sell Big Macs with beef in India, so they make them with chicken. But more important are the spices they use in their Indian menu. They've adapted it for the local market – the core brand is the same, but the food is Indian. That is where McDonald's has found traction.

There are 120 million Indian Internet users, around 10 per cent of the population, which isn't that high. What is unique is the way smartphone users go online. In India you don't need to buy a whole packet of cigarettes, you can buy singles; similarly, pre-paid Internet cards are selling like hot cakes here. For as little as 2 pence (3¢) you can go online for twenty minutes. Most marketers have realized that to penetrate the market here they need to reconfigure their brand, and the price point is vitally important. Whether you're selling

breakfast culture here in India – each state has its own traditional breakfast. So Kellogg's started talking to the children who would then grow up and eventually become parents themselves, and now everyone eats Kellogg's for breakfast, which I think sucks. I've seen India lose so much in the last fifteen years. The amount of boredom we had when we were growing up – I don't feel that today. Boredom is so important, it's when you get off your arse and do something to counteract or alleviate it; today you can't be bored.

The first wave of change here was the brands bringing in the content, and the second was reality TV. Imagine, we went from being clean – no foreign brands, no outside influences – to being saturated with global brands and reality TV in about ten years. I can't even understand what my parents are thinking when they watch TV.

cola or crisps or SIM cards or chewing gum, you need to deliver at a competitive price. The one thing that hadn't changed in India in the eighteen years I'd been away was how cheap the place is: the longest subway ride was 28p (44¢); a Pizza Hut Pizza £1.50 ($2.35); a cellphone charger £2 ($3.10); a text message was 0.1p. Taking this into consideration, the keys to the youth market are price, image and delivery. In that order.

For getting a message across, Bollywood is big and cricket is big. The most popular content downloads are Bollywood songs. India has 28 million Facebook users, and brands like Gillette have successfully created content for the site. However, fundamentally, brands in India are trying to seamlessly integrate with Bollywood movies on the screen, and then pick up that connection off-screen with consumer recall.

Interestingly, Hindi may be the national language, but it doesn't cut across the whole nation. There are more than one hundred different languages spoken in India, while English is used to unify the country in TV shows, commercials, radio and Bollywood films. English is not seen as the language of an ex-oppressor; it's viewed as international and a mark of education. This is an insight into how international brands have to adapt their products for a local market. It is the way forward. There is no one language to talk to the Indian youth. He or she is probably using a

My feeling is that Indian youth are going to reject the Western Internet and make their own version – whatever that will be. And that is scary. I don't think it's going to be about sneaker culture. I don't think it's going to be about the brands. It's going to be about what they can make. Bharat thinks of the modernized, slightly Western-influenced Indian (who grew up watching MTV) as a non-Indian, and India thinks of Bharat as backward. No matter where you go, you will find that both co-exist, and for some reason the rich are always India and the poor are always Bharat. It's a money thing. I hope that changes going forward. I think we need to change to become a small-town-led country, as the city-led culture is not really working in India."

"Advertising is entertainment; it's a commercial, it's thirty seconds of nonsense, and people treat it as such. One of the reasons people love advertising is because they get to mock it. Even

mixture of languages without even being aware
of it. So most global brands need to adapt their
means of communication. Smartphone and
cinema – that's how you reach them.

in places like Surat (a B-town) you will overhear
conversations where people are making fun of TV
commercials, which shows that they can filter out
the rubbish from the hard facts and then go to the
store and get a brochure and ask how many miles
to the gallon it does."

**Aids awareness adverts
masquerading as Bollywood
posters by AMO Group Bombay.**

Interview with a legend:
VIRAL PANDYA

"Samsung Phones with Mobile Tracker" from Out of the Box, New Delhi.

Viral is an Indian legend. If anyone understands
how to communicate with the Indian youth, Viral
does. He spent years as a top player in the Indian
advertising industry before starting his multi-
award-winning boutique agency, Out of the Box,
which continues to create consistently amazing
work. He has a small, select group of clients who
all love and trust him as if he were family. In return
he produces work that stands up on a global
stage and not only wins awards, but also (more
importantly) ensures the growth and success of
his clients' brands.

"Talk about India, and the first thing that comes
to mind is its population. It's humongous. What
we don't realize is that India, with a brigade
of 500 million people under 24, is also the
youngest country in the world. The youth of India
represents the youth of the world, which is what
makes them the quintessential global citizens.

We are in a boom. There is a lot of greed. This
country used to have a middle class. The father
worked, the mother stayed at home and the
kids studied. Now the father's working, so is the
mother, and the kids will have something going
on to make them money while they study.
Everyone is moving outside the house.

I may be 40 years old today but I think like an
18-year-old, which is rare. You have to engage
them; it can't be one-way. It's like a courtship
with a woman. You need to start having an affair.

A. R. Rahman, Sachin Tendulkar and Albert Einstein: all helping Indian youth to dream big.

72   283   Interview with a legend: ↓   Viral Pandya
Viral Pandya

These kids like engagements, unlike our parents, who used to swear by a product and be loyal to it; these kids are not loyal at all. They switch their girl- or boyfriends like they switch their brands. The upper-middle-class youth all use the iPhone, and they all want something that is a badge. They want to spend time mindlessly on Facebook for thirteen hours. While we are into advertising, the whole engagement with the young has to be interactive.

Viral's Indian Top Ten

1. Defining Indian youth: they are the ones who cannot live without the Internet. They don't spend much time on magazines and newspapers, but are extremely well read. They don't have time. They are the reason test cricket gave way to one day, and one day to Twenty20. For them, the word 'slow' doesn't exist. They are either fast or very fast.

They get bored easily. They started using their mobile phone at 12, which they change every six to seven months. They are independent. They want to stay away from parents even if they live in the same city. But they shy away from their responsibility. In a word, they don't give crap, or take it.

2. Marketing is tricky. You can't fool them. When it comes to youth, you no longer find a market for your products; you find a product for your market. You market with them, not to them. You can't buy their loyalty; you have to earn it.

3. The trick is to engage them, not to preach or talk down to them. Send them an SMS, tweet them, interact with them on Facebook, and the chances are you'll get them involved.

4. You can reach them without advertising, at least advertising in the conventional sense.

You've got to entertain them, and bring something new to their platter. Facebook didn't advertise. Neither did Google. They engaged them. The result is that they are big in India.

5. They are not as rebellious as the previous generation. They are cool if their parents use the same brands as they do, unless the parents don't poke their noses into their affairs. BlackBerry played it really well in India. With the TV commercial BlackBerry Boys, they positioned BlackBerry as a cool tool for the youth.

6. Big means nothing to them; being relevant means everything. Big Mac is not the biggest-selling brand in India. But among the best-selling items at McDonald's is McAloo Tikki Burger, their first local burger.

7. Often they are full of contradictions, too. Among the youth icons, you will find the richest

Indians – Anil Ambani, Sunil Mittal, etc. But the youth also support Anna Hazare, an anti-corruption crusader.

8. Their values are liberal. For example, adults will find the Fastrack commercials scandalous and shocking, but the youth lap them up.

9. Virgin Mobile is another brand that speaks the lingo of the youth. The people they portray in commercials are not goody-goody guys, but mischievous and roguish. Maybe one reason Nokia is losing its market share is because they no longer speak the idiom of the youth.

10. Make youth your brand ambassadors, treat them with respect, collaborate with them, and they can become your most effective asset in brand-building."

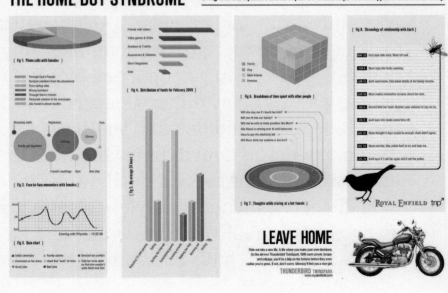

Motorbikes in India are usually sold in two
ways: by mileage (miles per gallon) and by
sex/Bollywood-esque appeal – "Buy this bike
and you'll get all the babes" kind of thing.
This campaign from Wieden+Kennedy Delhi
contradicted all of that and went for the jugular.

73 288 Royal Enfield ↓ Dan Berkowitz. Associate Creative Director, Wieden+Kennedy Delhi

"By highlighting a strong human insight and breaking the mould of traditional bike communications, the campaign resonated with the core audience and helped turn the Thunderbird into a cult brand for modern Indian youth. In India it's common for young men to live with their parents because of their folks' traditional mindset, even once they're married with children. The 'Leave Home' campaign gave a voice to a new generation seeking a more adventurous life and provided a solution in the form of the Thunderbird. Although it's tough to generalize in a country populated by over a billion people with so many different layers of society, the affluent and middle-class youth are driving the postmodern boom in India and want to be on a par with their peers globally when it comes to fashion, design and lifestyle. Cultural insights and a new sensibility in communicating have become powerful tools in inspiring the growing youth market."

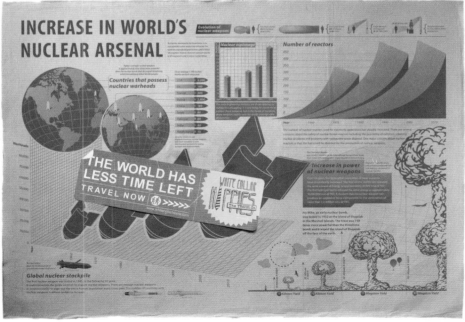

The White Collar Hippies campaign from
BBDO India is another breath of fresh air,
and announces a new kind of travel agency
for a new generation of Indian travellers.

"A country of many tongues united by one language – 'the language of action'. Indians never travelled very far from their homes in the past (school texts don't mention a single seafaring adventurer or a legendary admiral). In more recent times travel meant group tours accompanied by a cook to serve up vegetarian meals, or going to meet a relative in the West. Now they have embraced the spirit of adventure. A recent Bollywood hit, *You Only Live Once*, revolves around three friends on a road trip in Spain with a leap list (sky- and scuba-diving and running with the bulls in Pamplona). White Collar Hippies is a new-wave travel agency whose founders also share this need to discover oneself through travel. We are seeing postmodern, ironic communication like the WCH campaign finding increasing appeal with the youth, who don't want to be interrupted with commercial messages without at least being totally entertained."

291

Picky C is an ex-advertising creative director, who quit the industry to become one of the first Indian bloggers to understand how the blog can work as a powerful and indispensable tool to promote fashion. I spent a long lunch with her in a Tibetan restaurant in Gurgaon.

Designers Shivan & Naresh.
Shot by Parikhit Pal.

Where are Indian fashion blogs right now?

"India is getting there and is very hungry. A lot of blogs are just gossip – most just read like press releases. But people know stuff now, and a lot of the new bloggers are extremely passionate, and given the chance we will be better in a few years. Right now we're in a bit of a funny place, as fashion designers come and ask us, 'So what do you do? What's a fashion blogger? What does it mean?' And I'm like…oh great! The younger ones, the newer generation, are a little more clued-up and want to work with us and get us involved in their work from the beginning. But it's the older generation, some of the so-called established designers – they don't want to know; they behave like they don't need us. We don't need them either, it's just that sometimes we do seek some recognition from established names as well."

Designer Rimzim Dadu. Shot at Wills Lifestyle India Fashion Week.

Picky C –
Indian fashion blogger

↓ Picky C

Where is Indian fashion going? What would you like to see happen?

"What a lot of young designers are doing now is breaking out of the traditional Indian fashion route of designing saris and lehengas (the two traditional fashion staples for making money). They are trying to experiment and try new things, but unfortunately they never make the kind of money they would if they stuck to creating saris and lehengas. Take Sabyasachi – one of the premier designers in India right now. When he started out his whole approach was very vintage, very interesting. A couple of years into the business, he is now mostly doing saris and lehengas to make the money he wants to make. He's playing it safe, although you have to give him credit for beautifully marrying vintage and contemporary even while designing his Indian-wear collections. He is possibly the best-selling designer right now."

Designer Rimzim Dadu. Shot at Wills Lifestyle India Fashion Week.

Is there an Indian high street?

"No, unfortunately there are no good Indian high-street chains. We have Zara and Forever 21. The next step is to get a good Indian retail chain that we would be proud to go into. Right now they don't exist. The high-street shops are not respected; people won't buy if it's cheap. Indians like to show off, they want to pay for brands. Because of the new double-income, corporate jobs, people have way too much money and so they are going to malls and spending 20,000 rupees on imported brands just to tell their friends at work the next day. A lot of people shop abroad in Dubai or Singapore. What's interesting is when you mix imported and local: a Topshop skirt with an Indian necklace and a locally printed T-shirt from a street-wear designer and a tailored jacket from a market. I love that. But mass-market mainstream fashion is still dictated by Bollywood, and that's such a bad thing."

I spent some time talking to Ajai Jhala, CEO of BBDO India, about Indian advertising. It got interesting when I said I didn't think youth advertising is really about advertising any more, but more about creating content, putting on events, etc., and Ajai dropped the bomb and told me about his "I Feel Up!" campaign for 7Up, which is all about content.

The reasons to be cheerful are that India has the world's youngest population; it is a democracy; it has huge potential as a country with a healthy economy; sunshine helps; and there is a solid middle class. In countries with a large middle class, the people at the bottom have hope because they know they can be better and climb to the next rung, through education. So BBDO took that optimism and launched "I Feel Up!" through a Twitter-thon.

"Adapt, don't import. Initially the consumer in India found no appeal in the famous Omo [the Indian name of Surf detergent] campaign – 'Dirt is Good'. When the initial focus on the joy of play was shifted to getting dirty as a consequence of playing out, based in enduring values (filial piety, collective good, etc.), the core idea found deep resonance. Content needs to be embedded in a context. Brands like 7UP and Quaker have become part of the social conversation by embedding their content into the right context. Indians are among the most optimistic people in the world – a young democracy, growing middle class, new education and work opportunities, future rather than past orientation and significant headroom for growth in domestic consumption combine to create a buoyant sentiment.

7UP has started a movement to 'Bottle India's Optimism' through a series of interconnected activities under the theme of 'I Feel Up!' The campaign was kicked off virtually (#IFeelUp Tweet-a-Thon, which was the world's longest and possibly the largest virtual conference) and physically, as entrepreneurs and their students were refreshed by 7UP on board a train whose mission was to travel the length and breadth of the country to awaken the spirit of entrepreneurship among young Indians."

77

From Shanghai airport I took the Maglev train, the world's first commercially operated magnetic levitation train, which travels at 431 kilometres per hour as it flies over the old shacks and houses on the outskirts of the city. What does this have to do with anything? It shows how advanced China is, and how the old and the new thrive happily alongside each other. Once in the city I saw just how quickly and deftly China has adapted to the global economy without losing any of its unique identity. And this went double for the youth.

They were everywhere, an enormous market. From girls on the subway wearing glasses with no lenses doing a Chinese manga look, to skate-punk boys with a ton of tats, there were a lot of different youth styles rocked by both the coolest of the cool and the mainstream. Despite this nominally being a communist country, I discovered a totally free consumer market. But on the flip side, censorship is in full effect, and this is clearly visible in the lack of a Facebook or YouTube presence online. I can't say I missed them for the week or so I spent in China. However, from speaking to people working in the advertising industries I learned that there are always people watching to make sure you are not mocking or questioning the government.

Like in Russia (of which more later), youth advertising in China is still in its infancy, and, as in Brazil, the youth are ready for new experiences, whether real or digital. This is the perfect mindset

"Choosing a brand is a bit like having a democracy in a communist country. It's like that Malcolm X quote, 'If you don't stand for something then you'll fall for anything.' People want to connect to brands that are doing exciting and thrilling things that make them feel alive."

"In a lot of ways Chinese kids are not so different, but they are a bit more innocent. They are from a culture where advertising is relatively new and does not have a deep history like in the West. So people here are a lot less cynical about it, and are embracing consumption wholeheartedly. There is a kind of optimism and nationalism that you don't see so much in the Western world, and this brings a lot of power, more than they realize. Kids don't often know what to do with this. There is also so much choice now. You can buy any brand, any kind of phone, any shoe, and the more young people have that choice the more they want to believe in something. But they also understand

for advertisers to experiment with new ideas and methods of delivery – it is a great moment for progressive-thinking brands. By the time this book goes to press, according to the Data Center of China, more Chinese people will be buying smartphones than ordinary phones. This presents a golden opportunity to brands, while being something of a nightmare for the government, which often shuts down networks during public disturbances; the biggest mobile phone provider is China Mobile, a state-owned company with over 600 million users.

I went to a skate and music festival in the biggest skate park in the world, located in the far-eastern suburbs of Shanghai. The crazy thing was that the park is owned by the government. In between the skating, the punk bands, the free beer and the rain, a delegation of government officials took to the stage for a short presentation. None of the kids seemed to mind, and as soon as the oldies left the stage the party resumed with even more vigour.

In the West the youth are bored with traditional advertising, but in China they're not. Advertising is everything here (analogue, digital, online, offline) and they have their own versions of YouTube (Youku) and Twitter (Weibo), which have exploded in the past few years. The way Weibo has caught on here – over 250 million users – has opened China up, in the sense that people are

that every choice says a lot about who they are, that they stand for something and participate in different cultures – from skate to fashion to music. They have that power, and kids really want and need to identify with something. So brands become part of who or what they identify with."

"In this day and age, the Chinese youth are an enigma, but I do think technology is the most important factor in advertising. I grew up in a generation that straddled the line. I knew what it was like to be offline, to be without a smartphone and to be disconnected. Now, kids ONLY know connection, and have their first experience with a digital device much earlier than we ever did. I would like to think that this ability to be connected and informed online would make the job of selling to them more difficult, since they're more aware, but I'm not quite sure if that's true. For many people, the Internet and connectivity are less about learning and education than about finding a point of view and a voice with which to express themselves. In the West, Twitter is all about oversharing and hyper-linked journalism, but in China, Weibo is quite unique. And the whole concept of access – which wasn't there thirty years ago – be it access to a community online or access to brands, is really celebrated. This keeps the youth optimistic. It's also about what you're satisfied with culturally; "hungry" is a great way to describe the Chinese youth.

playing games and talking with friends. But I'm hearing conflicting reports of how children perceive advertising. In some ways, kids are smarter at finding out what is advertising, but I've also heard reports where children were given a game to play and only a minority could decipher whether or not it was marketing thinly disguised as a paid-for game."

Rob Campbell is the head of planning for
Wieden+Kennedy Shanghai, working on brands
such as Nike, Converse, Levi's and P&G, to
name a few. After a dodgy start as a session
guitarist for some of the worst 1980s pop stars,
he ended up working for – and starting – a bunch
of great companies in the UK, the US, Australia,
Singapore, Hong Kong and China. Rob is the
founder of homeless group Human_2, co-runs
the Global Advertising Planning School on the
web and is very, very pro-East.

Has consumption become intertwined with culture for the Chinese youth?

"A lot of people mistake this [consumerism] for naivety, as we've only had only ten or so years of this freedom, and it's fucking wonderful, it's like a whole new world. If you go back to where the West was at the same point in its evolution, I bet it was pretty much the same, but I think the division between the illusion of being part of the culture through consumption and the reality is a bit different here. In China people still buy to create an image. What's really interesting are their frames of reference, and you need to understand these if you're to make people feel something. In China the connection comes far more through physical experiences (what they call 'experiential' these days) rather than just advertising, the difference being that if you do it well (see Converse and Nike work), the youth will begin to believe in these brands. In the West most of the work was about making the youth think

the brands were great or cool, whereas here it's about making them believe in them…or making the youth think that they have a right to believe in them, and that's half the battle. Brands which can do this in a way that is actually meaningful (superficiality is in the eye of the beholder) will find that people react in a positive way.'

Analogue or digital? New or traditional media?

"TV in Asia is still a powerful medium for a bunch of different reasons, and yet so is digital. Digital has allowed the youth to gain a level of self-expression that culturally has been restrained – to the point where the government is going to act against it at some point. This is all to do with the middle class and their attitudes towards political integrity. Young people use Weibo almost like the speakeasies of the 1920s, where you could express yourself without fear of reprisal. Digital can provide the anonymity that gives them the

courage to speak out. Not in rebellious terms necessarily, but just personal expression – what many of us in the West might take for granted. Despite this, in some areas I think Chinese youth are incredibly well developed, just in different ways to their Western counterparts. In terms of their ability to be quite open to new ideas I think they're developed, at least in areas like fashion.

As an old fucker I get to relive my youth again as I see through my eyes what is happening in their lives and how it makes them feel. It's amazing and exciting and pretty infectious. The Chinese youth are one of the most brand-literate generations on the planet. In all honesty, if you want something here, you can get it, and tech has allowed them to know which brands to have and which brands to avoid."

How does censorship affect your day-to-day working?

"I think that censorship helps define whether you care or not. It's easy to get hold of a lot of superficial information, but if you want to dig deeper to find real depth – depending on the subject – you're going to have to really look for it. And if you want to find original or niche cultures, then the fact that censorship is so entrenched here means the people who go out and search for it are basically legitimate followers of that culture because it requires real effort to go get it.

We face censorship on the language and the iconography. Unofficial public events (like flash mobs) are seen as a political rally. From a commercial perspective you can't say, 'Fuck the system' (and very few would want to do that anyway), but in some ways there's a perverse pleasure in being given a load of barriers to get through – it makes you try that bit harder to find

something that's really great and can be made
to work. Sure, we've failed at times, but when
you get it happening and see what it means and
and what it does, it's exciting. You have to think
broadly, because if you pin all your hopes on one
key visual or event and then that doesn't happen,
you're back to the drawing board. This market
moves faster than Superman and time cannot be
wasted. Essentially we are here to help our clients
make more money, and we believe they can do
it in two ways: 1. You can brainwash people with
masses of media, or 2. You can inspire them to
want to be a part of what you're doing because it
represents who they are or what they believe. We
choose the latter here. We want to attract rather
than chase."

Who do you think is doing interesting work in China?

"The greatest strategists on the planet are the Chinese government, and I'm not being facetious, I genuinely believe this. Obviously I don't agree with everything they do but I'm in awe in their ability to be intellectually devious, and in some respects you have to have some of that cheekiness to get stuff under the radar here. People don't really like rebellion in China, not generally – people love this country – but by creating an infrastructure that gives them a voice, albeit within the lines of the law, they're going to embrace the moment rather than say, 'Fuck everything!' At least that's what normally happens. Basically we create structures that let people be free within them, and that's when you get some great stuff. If you try to stage-manage it, then it doesn't work."

79

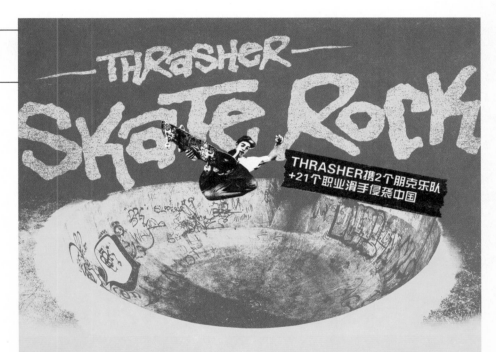

Over the last few years Converse China has been quietly creating some of the finest youth advertising/communications in the world, and consistently producing original events. As global skateboarding enters its eighth decade, in China the sport is only ten years old, if that, and with around 50,000 Chinese youth regularly skating (many not starting until their twenties, given the pressure to focus on studies), skateboarding is not only in its infancy but is a fledgling hobby at best. Despite this, Converse has chosen to make this free-spirited, independent sport a pillar of its China marketing story since 2009, selling a fair few pairs of skate shoes in the process, but more importantly inspiring tens of millions of young people across the country.

In 2008, Converse bought back its China business from its local license partner, and set about positioning the brand in line with the key global pillars of independent music, art, fashion and skateboarding. But rather than simply playing on Converse's global heritage in skateboarding, the newly formed China marketing team set out to understand what "independence" means to youth consumers on the mainland.

Discussions with the Chinese skate community and other creative leaders drew a clear conclusion that local context is far more important than global provenance when telling stories of the growing "independent spirit" among Chinese youth. Having brought in local skate pioneer

"I think Converse is the first company to treat their skaters as stars rather than just skate kids. Converse respects skateboarding; that's very important! They spotted the right skaters to work for them. They did the right skate things (party, video, tour) in the right skate way."

"Converse quickly realized that for skateboarding to really take off in China someone needed to foster the industry at the centre among core skaters, while inspiring young Chinese kids with the free-spirited ethos that skating represents. Everyone is totally inspired by the skate team, trips, events and films that Converse China have done so far – it's all generating a lot of good will for the brand, and a lot of pride among the local creative communities."

Eric Lai as its skate manager, Converse China built a local pro team, drawing four top riders from across the country. In 2010 the team journeyed into the middle of China to discover new skate spots, while musing about a sport they felt was both an expression of their own independence and an analogy for the journey of self-discovery that Chinese youth are on. The film, Ni (Change the Game), shot by duo Patrik Wallner and Anthony Claravall, has been viewed by tens of millions of young people throughout the country, with many sharing how inspired they have been by the film's theme of pursuing your dreams.

Throughout 2010 and 2011, the support that Converse China put behind skateboarding among the growing legion of skaters could be seen from the trips they undertook and filmed throughout China, Thailand, Vietnam, the USA and, most recently, Mongolia. Like Ni, the Mongolia film, Where Do We Land (also by Wallner and Claravall), sent a message of discovery and independence to skaters and beyond, reinforcing that Converse China wants all young Chinese to be inspired by the creativity that skateboarding represents.

Converse China remains committed to fusing skateboarding with art, design, music and fashion, as seen from the summer 2011 series of "Block Party" events, and their partnership with global skate mag Thrasher to host a multi-team

On the road with the Converse China team.

"With *Ni* and then *Where Do We Land,* Converse China has successfully tapped into a core dream of hundreds of millions of young people across China – the desire to forge their own path and to create their own future. *Where Do We Land* was 100 per cent made-by-skaters: director, editor, producer, talent…everything. PR goes to hell, as only skaters really know about *Where Do We Land*! That brings the message that Converse believes Chinese skaters can be the best, and only those guys can do it."

"King of the Road" skate trip and a multi-band "Skate Rock" music tour across the country.

The key to broadcasting these messages to a much wider audience has been Converse's focus on nurturing (and creating) digital communities across the country. These deep roots into the huge number of social media sites in China have built an online audience for Converse of over 100 million creative youth. In doing this they have been able to take skateboarding from a grassroots activity to a nationwide topic of discussion. Skateboarding remains a hugely popular sport around the world, and its rise has just begun in China. With brands like Converse getting behind skateboarding and skateboarders and, more importantly, telling the story of the "skater lifestyle" to the immense Chinese youth population, it's fair to assume that one day China might have the world's largest skateboard industry. This can only be a good thing for early pioneer brands like Converse.

"When Converse brought *Thrasher* mag to China they pulled off something that was long needed, bringing together the entire pro skate scene to compete in 'King of the Road', and capping it off with an insane 'punk meets skate' series of nearly out-of-control demos and gigs from one end of China to the other."

"I don't skateboard but I can see that the free spirit of the skateboarders is something that can inspire me to follow my own creative dreams."

Customizing a classic pair of Chucks.

80

NeochaEDGE is a creative agency that represents some of the most talented artists, designers and musicians in China via its EDGE Creative Collective. The work that the agency and the collective produce has one common theme – it talks directly to the youth with its edge and attitude. It's not rocket science to figure out that many of China's agencies and brands are beating a path to NeochaEDGE's door.

The firm started as Neocha and has since grown into one of the most sought-after agencies in China. Today the team regularly turn down work as they are too busy. They only take on projects that fit their vision, which is something that I applaud wholeheartedly: only do work that you understand or believe in. NeochaEDGE makes this work happen, first as a creative agency that comes up with ideas for a client, then turning these ideas into reality using their internal team and a roster of designers and artists, before producing the final product through their network of technical guys. A real one-stop shop.

"We started out in 2007 as a social networking platform (we were simply called Neocha then: www.neocha.com) catering to young Chinese creative talent: visual artists and musicians. We had hoped to get 20,000 users but soon got much more than that, which created a problem in terms of bandwidth costs. We thought we could execute some sort of advertising model and sell ad space on the site to pay the bills, but it didn't really work out like that. When we talked to different brands and media companies, they thought the site was amazing, but weren't impressed with our user and traffic numbers – these were the only things they really cared about at the time. They all told us to talk to their creative and production departments as we were sitting on a goldmine of creatives – an extensive pool of young talents who were making compelling visual arts and music content. So we began to rethink our model and talk to brands and agencies about projects that would allow us to tap the community for content creation.

Adidas by Honghua.

We did a variety of test projects and found it to be fun, interesting and rewarding for us and the artists in our collective…and, most importantly, it made money for everyone."

"We've had some of our ideas rolled out by other companies and sometimes it just didn't work. So to take the idea from concept to production is ideal, as we can tightly control the quality and make sure it's the best it can be. Our clients are brands such as Nike, Absolut, Disney, Coach, Adidas and Puma, and we work with their respective design teams on projects, from installations in their offices, to garment and product customizing, iPad apps, viral videos and in-store animations. We design and create pretty much any content you can think of in the visual arts space, some physical, some digital. Either way, someone always needs it and we produce it."

81

Hong Kong-based Hypebeast leads the way in all things streetwear and beyond! I spent some time with its founder, Eugene Kan, and drilled him for his insider's view on youth. Hypebeast began as a site that mainly covered sneakers, but it has diversified immensely over the last few years. It has gone further and further in different directions, and while the love for sneakers hasn't changed, the site has now created a significantly wider range of content. In its use of blogging as a promotional tool, Hypebeast provides a great example of content and commerciality working in perfect harmony.

"Hypebeast is probably considered many things, but predominantly we're an online magazine that focuses on various facets of fashion, including street wear, high fashion, street culture and everything in between. We essentially scour all corners of the globe and the Internet for the latest fashion-related news for our viewers. We've become a pivotal member of the online and fashion communities for our ability to deliver interesting news to our readers. In addition, we have a strong list of bloggers who offer insights and opinions on industry-relevant matters. Capping everything off is a forum that allows many global members to interact, communicate and participate in a focused environment.

Air Jordan XIV Pizza Box.

Fifth anniversary Bearbrick :CHOCOOLATE Toy.

I think it's a transitional time for youth advertising right now. The people occupying the boardrooms are still from a generation even beyond myself who had technology thrust upon them in a less organic way. When I picked up a computer, I was still young and could slowly learn how to use it. It wasn't a crash course, it was an everyday occurence, whereas past generations may have been in the middle or start of their working careers and have had to learn a new and difficult set of skills to remain relevant. When people who have grown up having a full and organic digital experience enter the boardroom, that's when youth advertising will be at its strongest, as they understand the concept much better."

319

The best way to get your head around something is to dive in and try to fathom it; see if you can swim, as it were. After a baptism of fire, getting completely lost on the Metro and streets of the capital a few times, I discovered that Moscow is mentally and culturally disconnected from the rest of Russia, which in turn considers itself separate from Europe: these are the vital pieces of information needed to ensure an honest perspective on a fascinating emerging market.

The first contradiction (always a sign that something interesting is about to happen) is that the Russian youth of today are unconsciously connected to the old Soviet Union, through the lives and experiences of their parents and grandparents, but they want to get out there and experience as much of the new world as they can – only on their terms. They are very stubborn; I discovered that this is a very Russian trait! I spent an afternoon wandering along Arbat Street (the equivalent of Oxford Street or 42nd Street) and checked the youth out: from getting wasted drinking vodka and apple juice at one end, to the usual getting off with the opposite sex with your mates taking the piss at the other, it all seemed pretty standard, but the Russians do it their own way – hardcore, all or nothing, which is also how the wealth seems to be distributed here. Life for the Russian youth is all about experience. There is a lot of drinking going down. Beer has only just been classified as alcohol – before, it was just a

82

320   **Russia – Moscow**   ↓ **Luis Tauffer. Creative Director, BBDO Moscow**

"I think that the global youth are quite uniform, for the obvious reasons – globalization, Internet, etc. – but because we have had some differences in the recent past here in Russia, we need to understand where this generation is coming from. They have inherited sincerity from their grandparents and entrepreneurial skills from their post-Soviet parents, who started new lives and businesses after the collapse of communism. Add the individualism of today's role models, and you have the Russian youth.

This entrepreneurial heritage, along with the insecurity that they feel about the future (Russia has changed so much recently and had so many crises that people are sceptical) is creating a fearless generation who think they can do everything and are not afraid to try new things. I was supposed to hire a 23-year-old guy to work on some big brands. During the interview, it felt like I was looking for a job, because actually he

beverage. There are kiosks on every street corner selling it. Outside of the cities there are problems with Russian moonshine, called Samogon, which is made out of sugar, beet, potato, corn, anything – even plywood – which I must admit I didn't try.

One strange thing is that there are two rates of pay in Moscow: one for those born in the city and one for those who aren't. I thought this was a bit strange, but that's how it goes down. You get less if you're not born into the privilege of Moscow. And before you ask, they always check. I also discovered that there are two types of Russia: the Virtual Russia – how the government sees it – and the Real Russia, how it is on the Internet. Consumers have high spending power, as there is a low rate of tax (15 per cent) across the board, low rent/mortgages thanks to the high quantity of public housing, and the average working youth has a high disposable income of around £12,000 ($19,000) after they've paid out for the necessities. And the Russians like to spend! I was immediately struck by how everything is on display, like a giant shop window: affluence, money, international super-brands. The more the merrier, the bigger the better. There is a Louis Vuitton flagship store now in Red Square, which just about sums it up for me. In Moscow, excess is the norm and there is no end to the bombardment of aspirational goals.

I took to the road with a friend who is a Russian "pop star" (unlike in the West, they still exist in

was posing all the questions to me, trying to find a reason to accept the job that he was looking for! One day later, he called me to say that he wouldn't take the job, as he had his blog to run, and this would probably be more interesting for him. So, basically, a young creative has a chance to enter a big company, work for big clients, and start to build a career…exactly what my generation had in mind. But he thinks that this might be boring and prefers to work on something by himself that gives him pleasure and more freedom, even without being sure if it would give him any stability in the future. And he is not embarrassed to admit it. I think this example pretty much shows what I am talking about. At that moment I didn't like his attitude. But I confess I wish I had this sense of freedom."

"The Russians have their own minds. There is no overall difference, but some of the parts are different. For example, they didn't get the

Russia) and got to see the youth up close and personal. They seem to love the fact that now there is a whole division of advertising aimed especially at their demographic. Before 1990 there was no youth advertising at all, and outside of Moscow and St Petersburg this has to be taken into consideration. The other cities are still playing cultural catch-up, and this is where the majority of the audience lives.

Effective campaigns rely heavily on social networking and radio to engage their target. The big social networking sites are Vkontakte, Odnoklassniki and Mail.ru, with Facebook coming fourth (it will probably be number one by the time you read this). Twitter hasn't taken off as much

as in the rest of the world; it appears they think it's boring. Twitter is just 145 characters of text, whereas the attitude here is all about the image. They want to show off: flash cars with very strange paint jobs; designer label on top of designer label; they want to stand out by any means necessary. Everything is excessive, and "Show, don't tell" is the mantra of the Russian youth.

Diesel 'Be Stupid' campaign. In Moscow, yes, they got it, but outside, in the country and other towns and villages, it was too hard for them to understand; they don't know what it means. Regional advertising is extremely poor and very boring, and they don't see a huge amount of advertising – they don't have much experience of being consumers. We've just started doing some interesting work aimed at the youth in the last decade. Outside of Russia, people are used to youth advertising and culture – they've seen it for years – but there are no subcultures here. Even now people don't want to be individuals, they don't know how to stand out. They are not watching great films, they look at reality TV like *Dom-2*, and emulate the casual problems and stupid ideas they see on the screen. With subcultures, if you stand out with tattoos and black hair outside of the cities you will just be seen as a freak and you won't make friends with anyone. There is not much recreational drug culture, as drinking

Russian aesthetics right now.
By Dopludo Collective.

is so much cheaper. No one here is creating anything around drugs. They go to parties and don't care if they drink or take drugs – it makes no difference. Kids begin to drink here around 14 years old."

"The main problem is that back in Soviet times people had no identity. You were supposed to be like everyone else, and you had this huge mass of people who had no aspiration for any individuality – everyone had the same food, clothes, furniture and goals. Now it's all changed, and when the new generation popped up they didn't remember any of this, but the old mentality is subconsciously transferred onto them. They are very open to all new things – like advertising. They are copying without knowing it. The weird thing is that they know what they want to do before they turn 21. They are in a hurry, as they feel that time is slipping away, but on the other hand they are a little bit lazy as they have it all

↓ **Anna Pushkareva**
↓ **Anton Demakov.**
  Creative, Saatchi & Saatchi Moscow

compared to the previous generation. I think the Internet gives them the illusion of having way too many opportunities, which makes them very self-obsessed and always thinking of how they will look in their Facebook photos."

"The first time I met Apple it blew my mind. When I was a kid I worked on a PC and when I first got to the agency and got my first Mac – wow! Another moment is when McDonald's appeared in Moscow in the 1990s. This was the first taste of Western culture we had, and I remember the queues down the street, and the taste of the food stayed with me. It was a special moment."

83 ³²⁵

Walking around Moscow, I noticed that
the pavements were covered in stencil
advertisements for youth-related events,
websites and products. I discovered that
this was illegal but tolerated, and it seemed
like a good starting point for examining
the advertising and emerging cultures.
Youth advertising is literally coming up
from the streets here.

84

The Boroda Project, the most progressive and forward-thinking agency in Moscow, really understand the youth, as they are all young themselves – it is a group of five award-winning creatives (plus a handful of freelancers) who have previously worked in the usual big-name agencies in Moscow. At some point, they realized that the best ideas are not constrained to just one medium or one channel of output, and so they set up Boroda (Russian for "beard") as an ideas agency that would use all means necessary to spread the word of its clients and projects. One of their projects is Story Store, a concept-led brand and shop with a completely new approach: all the items on sale have an emotional value. Every object has its own unique history and backstory, and is accompanied by an online video as evidence, linked by a QR code that can be scanned by any smartphone and then watched instantly. It is a great link between the artists who create the stories, and the culture of the commercial world. Examples of the stories include:

– A teddy bear that had a private lap dance.
– A shirt from a comic-book character.
– The most musical sneakers, worn by a support act who performed before the headliner.
– A summer collection of swimsuits that have had a dip in the Arctic Ocean.
– A designer dress made from white fabric pieces, all collected from different cultures.
– Posters made by musicians who used their bodies to stamp the ink.

"Our ethos is that it is stupid to limit our lives and our minds just to advertising. We can help brands, but they need to trust us. We have had a calm period for a while, after the huge cultural change. There are no new fashion designers, or writers, or artists coming out of Russia. We have a lot of genius people but they are too young. We need our talented people to come back, as in the 1990s they all left to work in Europe and the US. I don't think they believed in the Russian government. With Story Store, first we found the insight: we value not material things but the impressions and memories connected with them. So we decided to fill items with emotional value and make a trend out of it. It's an interesting experiment, which we believe can be a business platform as well. It's an opportunity for young artists or musicians to promote themselves in a non-standard way, a nice human media platform for brands, and later on, an opportunity for people to show their creativity and earn some money."

STORYSTORE

Buttons #1
watched the whole
Lynch collection
in one breath
New York 2011

85

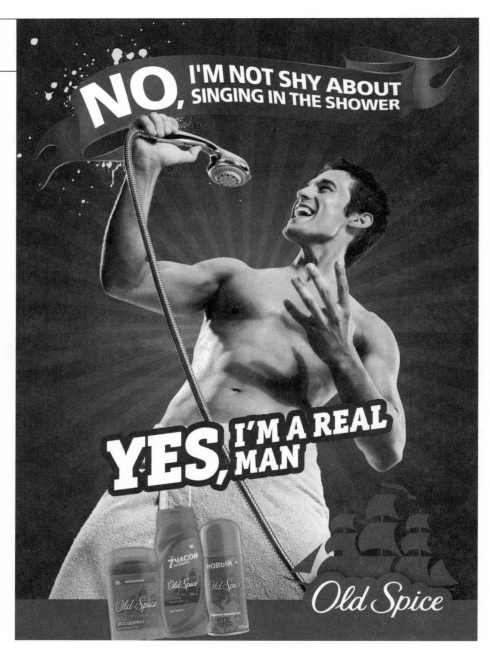

Old Spice in Russia is a great example of how a
local campaign can be just as effective as a global
one, even when it is up against a very successful
global campaign, such as 'The Man Your Man
Could Smell Like', starring the unique talents
of Mustafa!

"To promote Old Spice in Russia we decided to
create something new and extraordinary for the
Russian market. We wanted to hit the young guys.
It was very interesting as we created the group
via [social media site] Vkontakte, and quickly got
100,000 people. It was so fast. It worked because
it was a conversation with the Russian youth. We
knew the messages were getting through, and
we engaged them, and we could see how many
people were using the deodorant every day. It
was not so Russian, but it was all about being the
'real man', which is quite Russian. We asked them
to show images and videos of how Russian their
lives were, by encouraging them with virals
we shot – this set them free…"

86

A couple of months after I'd finished writing this book I spent a weekend in Dublin at the OFFSET creative festival and got to spend some quality time with Erik Kessels. I've written about Erik before, and, as you'll know, he's included at the beginning of this book. But the stuff you can't bottle is about taking advantage of the unexpected, and this is why I had to include these words from the most creative, exciting, adventurous and courageous man in the industry. If there is anyone who defines youth advertising, it's Erik. There was once a bit of graffiti that proclaimed, "Clapton is God"; in my book, Kessels is God. To get the ball rolling I threw out the idea that "there are no rules and no one knows anything", which is something I firmly believe in.

"To be creative you need to be constantly insecure. There are no rules for anything. When we talk about the future of advertising, we're really asking what is the future of the way people think, or what is the future of ideas. If you have a great media-independent idea, that will always survive the trends. I find advertising agencies in general – even though I work in one – extremely old-fashioned and opportunistic. I can't believe that the world's agencies still give awards to each other – only the hairdressing industry gives out more awards. Over the past fifteen years, nothing has gone out of the door that I hated. We like to do good work and work with brands, but there is a limit to that relationship. When they try to force us to do something that's really stupid or dumb, I just stop working for them. It's quite painful sometimes. Once we had to do it with a client that was 60 per cent of the agency's income, and the next few months were a bit dry…"

Bavaria Beer handbook for men.

Why is 95 per cent of advertising seen by the public as shit?
Why does the volume of TV spots go up when everyone in the
world hates that, and it doesn't make anyone rush out to buy?

"This is down to the fact that clients, focus groups and directors of companies want to be comfortable. Uncomfortable advertising is already touching something different; I mean uncomfortable in a good way. Agencies are very conservative. They look inside instead of out. It's only about money, it's about getting bought by another agency. There are not a lot of ideals in the industry. To be creatively successful in advertising you really have to hate advertising. I really hate advertising, and I think everyone does – 95 per cent is horrible, but it's that 5 per cent that drives me. Underwear advertising always looks the same; car advertising always looks the same, and it's nice to try and change that. The successful work is usually the one that challenges what has come before."

How do you deal with a client that simply doesn't get the work; that can't see what you're doing is best for their brand?

"You either compromise, or you don't. I'd rather not, but there are a lot of agencies that will. My life is too short to spend with assholes. You know if you like the client from the start. If you go against your gut, then the relationship will just fall apart after a few months anyway. I think creatives and clients should spend more time sitting around in bars chatting about shit. Meeting rooms are not the best places to get to know a person, to develop a relationship. When I look back, some of my best work was done with people who I had the best relationship with. You need to put the effort in, you need to invest. But also sometimes the client doesn't need to work with an asshole of an agency."

I've learned so much writing this book, my mind has been completely blown apart. Like anyone with any form in the youth demographic, I thought I knew it all, but the older I get, the less I realize I actually know. One thing I am certain of is that Internet 2.0 has created something new – Advertising 2.0 – especially when it comes to selling to the youth.

Things done changed, to quote Biggie Smalls, and for the better, for the good. This is our second Summer of Love; our Stonewall; our Industrial Revolution. And what great timing, as advertising outside of the youth market has, in my humble opinion, reached a point of stagnation. Never has the output been seen as so annoying; there is

some real hatred and resentment building in the public psyche about what is being pumped out on commercial TV and printed on the pages of Hello! magazine. This is one of the reasons why it's great to be working in youth advertising, where the alternative scenario prevails: make a connection and there isn't hatred, only love for the brand.

As we all know, the first great revolutionary moment for advertising was when Bill Bernbach moved the art director two floors down into the same room as the copywriter, and got them to bounce ideas off each other to come up with fresh ones. This became the creative bedrock of our industry, from which advertising grew into what it used to be – before the World Wide Web changed

"For me, 'advertising' is an aloof, even strangely ennobling term. It has connotations of red braces and glass offices overlooking Madison Avenue – whereas what KesselsKramer has always tried to do is talk to people, nothing more. Sometimes how we talk is weird, sometimes challenging, sometimes charming, sometimes confrontational. I admire anyone who shares that philosophy. The ultimate master of this type of communication is Andy Warhol. He did it better than any of us, and he didn't even have a Facebook page."

everything. The next revolution will not only be televised, it will also be streamed, flash-mobbed (cringe), Flickr'd, YouTube'd and festival'd.

Right now the world's creative eyes are wide open to any suggestions about what works and (more importantly) what sells – though without obviously selling, or being seen as selling. One part of selling to the youth has become a mission of infiltrating whatever subcultures or creative disciplines you think will best suit the brand. In my humble opinion, the only way to do this is by being as open as possible. Any one of these kids we're attempting to sell to is so much smarter than the average ECD or CEO it hurts, and they can spot an old fool in youth's trainers a mile off (or a second into a YouTube clip or from a brief glance at a fly poster). The youth are in control of the brands, not vice versa.

Thanks to the digital revolution, advertising has become the last bastion of true creativity. It's the only discipline where events, workshops, music, writing, and still and moving imagery come together as one experience. Movies and, to some extent, music videos used to do this, but not any more – not since the accountants took over the creativity and killed it, and MTV spun off into reality TV. To this creativity, add some user intervention, outdoor experience and the odd guerrilla stunt, and there you have an unbeatable combination. You can slave away spending your

87   338   The future –
The stuff you can bottle   ↓ **George Monbiot. Author
and investigative journalist**

"Advertising claims to enhance our choice, but it offers us little choice about whether we see and hear it, and ever less choice about whether we respond to it. Since Edward Bernays began to apply the findings of his uncle Sigmund Freud, advertisers have been developing sophisticated means of overcoming our defences. In public they insist that if we become informed consumers and school our children in media literacy we have nothing to fear from their attempts at persuasion. In private they employ neurobiologists to find ingenious methods of bypassing the conscious mind."

life savings on a short film that no one apart from a few geeks at an obscure film fest will see, but make one TV spot and it's there with an audience of millions. Or why not bypass the traditional media completely and get something tactile going that then rolls over onto Vimeo/YouTube and for a nanosecond sets the interweb on fire? This is just a small element of what promoting brands has become, and this is why it's such an amazing industry to work in right now. The world is yours for the taking; all you have to do, as a creative or strategist or client or tea-boy/girl, is get involved.

For me, as the new breed of creative director, the ideal brief is to work with brands who will let me create great content or become involved with subcultures, and will not necessarily insist on having a logo revealed at the end – if at all. This would reflect back on the brand as being far-sighted and progressive, and would push creativity to the next level. We need brands to take this long view, so that they become naturally synonymous with whatever culture they are nurturing, which would lead to unheard-of levels of brand loyalty. "But they have to show their logo!" I hear you traditional ad men shout, and this is where you are showing your age, and perhaps your ego. The brand needs to step back and listen rather than talk, then allow this information slowly to become the DNA of the creative, which will continue to promote the brand in whatever content is relevant. Even then

"I don't know – yet – where advertising is going. I don't think I want to know where it's going. We are like a marriage agency and we have to make people fall in love with brands. I don't care how we get this message across. We just have to be flexible to the new ways of delivery. There is no need to complicate things. Advertising is really quite simple: you have to be able to connect and engage, but you also have to love to do it. Different things, weird things. What has changed is how we put that message out."

you don't need to show the logo. If you make something for a sports brand, no one needs to be dipped head-to-toe in it; if the idea is great, it will work without the product being shown in every other frame. I know this may be hard for you to swallow, but that's because it is a message from the future: the bigger the brand, the bigger the risk, the bigger the pay-off.

Culture is merging with commerce. Perhaps in a few years we won't be able to tell where one ends and the other begins. It is vital that brands understand and get involved (as much as they can) in the cultures and subcultures that make up the world of youth. The future of youth advertising isn't going to be about "adverts", as the whole definition of what advertising does has now changed. The advertising industry is still based on a very old ecosystem that has been extended and extended and extended, because the people running it know how to make money out of it. But this system is extinct. The idea of "the medium is the message" came from the fact that a message gained importance from being on TV or on a ninety-eight-sheet poster. This doesn't work any more. The message has changed direction – it's now coming from the audience, towards the brands, and the word coming back is "Engage me, add something to my life, make me better, or fuck off!" These words have to be taken seriously. Advertising is close to becoming a bridge between commerce

---

87 340 **The future –**   ↓ **Steve Henry**
         The stuff you can bottle   ↓ **Bill Hicks. Comedian**

"Youth advertising is the best place to work, because it gives you the best opportunity to experiment. And that's what creativity is all about – experimenting, trying something new. If you think you've got the answer, you're not being creative. Being creative is about being in a place where you don't know the answer."

"The world is just a ride, but we always try to kill those good guys who try and tell us that, you ever notice that? And let the demons run amok. But it doesn't matter because it's just a ride. And we can change it any time we want. It's only a choice. No effort, no work, no job, no savings and money. A choice right now between fear and love. The eyes of fear want you to put bigger locks on your doors, buy guns, close yourself off. The eyes of love, instead, see all of us as one."

and culture, a walkway between the brand, the consumer and the subculture: music, art, creativity, sports and special interests.

Nobody really knows anything – this is the only point to start from. But advertising is a brutal business, and you have to keep innovating, evolving and recreating yourself or you will become extinct. This goes for creatives as much as for brands – you're only as good as your last ad. Some of the largest youth brands out there refused to have anything to do with this book, not for personal reasons, but because they don't allow any reproduction of comment on their advertising. Apple, Coke, Uniqlo... all declined for their work to be included, which I found rather strange, as

what is the sole purpose of advertising? It's a funny old game if you think about it. I'll leave you with this thought: for the first time in history, in the West, the teens are now outnumbered by the older generation. This is vitally important. The money and power seem to lean towards the grey end of the spectrum, which is a bad thing for the youth. But all the important and influential youth movements and subcultures were born out of adversity, out of struggle. This is exactly what the youth needs to keep producing fresh culture – something to fight against. And the youth are certainly getting their backs pushed against the wall.

Va$hti in downtown
Johannesburg, 2011.

Think about it. Differently.

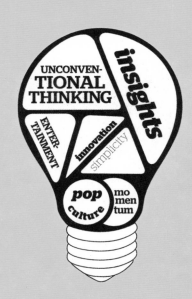

88

"The spirit of youth, the stuff you can't bottle, is
the first night out on a holiday away with your
mates; a 17-year-old street-style hustler from
Durban telling it like it is on his blog; a sample
of a classic hook regurgitated and remixed
into something that sounds like the zeitgeist
of the moment; a style or fashion that has been
customized in a bedroom in front of a mirror
in a shitty, tragically boring suburb somewhere;
it's a lyric that strikes the heart and changes
your life for ever; a photograph or a film
or a passage from a novel that says
something to someone about their
life; it's a shared experience, a
moment in time when everything
just clicks and the pieces fall into
place and everything is all right
– perfect, even: the sun shines,

the music plays, the drugs work, eyes catch one another across a space filled with movement, rhythm and joy, and then, just for a second, a light shines on a face and something strikes your heart and this is a moment that will stay with you for ever. And that's not just the drugs talking either. It's a rough stony beach where some friends sit and throw stones at a plastic Evian bottle floating in the sea. A joint is sparked, smoked and passed. The sun begins to set, a plane drops low as it banks over the coast just before it lands. The sea merges with the sky and you have to look away, and just then a car drives past with the windows open and the music pumping. You follow the music. The city comes alive at night and it's into this playground that you wander.... For this is where the true spirit lives."

King Adz

The Magic Triangle: Fast Cheap Good

This can be applied to every piece of work created in advertising, especially relevant to youth work as the client will always want it fast and cheap.

You can only ever pick two sides of the triangle on any brief: Fast + Cheap = Not Good. Fast + Good = Not Cheap. Good + Cheap = Not Fast.

The Ten Commandments (The Youth Testament)

1. There are no rules and nobody really knows anything
This is so true. This is the best place to start. If you come from nothing, then anything is possible. The golden rule is that if you think the client will never go for your idea, then it's probably the best one for the brand. Just like the movie, music and TV industries – nobody really knows what works.

2. Research your market/subculture
Begin the project with some truly transparent, inspirational, research. Some anthropological research into human behaviour will help you to understand your target, your co-conspirators, and ultimately your brand. Then you can begin to work out what you should be saying (see point 6). Understand the sub/culture you want to become part of and begin contributing something meaningful. The long game will pay off. No quick bucks, no short cuts!

3. Content is king
Authentic content is the conduit between brand and audience; it's what makes a live connection. True content has to be a by-product of street and original culture; of exciting, interesting and weird-and-wonderful events that happen on or near the street. It can't be the usual brand exercise that has been written, story-boarded, focus-tested, rinsed, strung out to dry, then packaged up with a logo and chucked out into the world. Selling to the youth isn't about telling them to buy. It's about integrating your brand into their world. One of the best ways to do this is by producing relevant and engaging content. Documentaries, shows, exhibitions, books, magazines, workshops...

4. Capture the spirit
If you successfully capture the spirit of youth (the stuff you can't bottle) then your communications will have more chance of working. I know this is easier said than done, but this is what I've tried to show (not tell) in the 352 pages of this book. This is when you can take advantage of the fact that

advertising has become content. This is when you really need to tap into the power of the narrative.

5. Take some massive risks
I've seen this so many times. The brand/client/agency doesn't want to make any mistakes. Nothing of any worth is ever achieved by not taking risks. The best work comes out of the unknown, commonly known as the risk/reward equation. This is the only way forward. There is absolutely no point in doing lame work; it will be a waste of your time and their money

6. Always ask: "What am I saying? What am I doing? And why should they care?"
Make the message relevant and concise. You will only have a very limited window of opportunity to engage. Then make sure the project means something. Forget selling fame – the "star-maker" syndrome is dead in the water. What matters is community and meaning. "What am I saying?" (about the brand), and '"Why should they care?" (about the brand). If – like Morrisey said – the piece of advertising you've created 'Says nothing to me about my life' then you know you've gone wrong somewhere.

7. You can't fake it – be honest and be authentic
If you can't create something solid from the above six points, hire someone who can. There are a million talented designers/art directors, writers, photographers, directors, etc., waiting for a break. Start with a youthful, broad team, and allow their enthusiasm to influence everything you do.

8. No logo
Don't run the logo unless you absolutely have to. Don't put gratuitous unexplained product shots in brand-sponsored docs about culture. Despite what you may think, advertising isn't about the logo any more. I know there are a lot of dinosaurs out there who will get annoyed by this, but that's the truth. Adapt or die. Word of the brand will always rise to the top, albeit slowly, but surely, and this is what the brand needs: some proper word of mouth that can only be created by decent content.

9. If the client doesn't trust you, then get another client

The days of the client ruling are over, especially in the youth market. The client knows less than you (see previous point) and this should tell you something. If they know more than you, they wouldn't be in the same room. They'd be doing it themselves – or trying to. If they don't believe in you then walk away; this has to be a marriage of equal partners.

10. Use the right language (vernacular is so hard to get right) – use word of mouth.

Never get lean (which actually means get high) on your own supply. Always tell it like it is, regardless of the risk. Don't trim or modify the message because you're scared that you may lose the account. And when this message is going out, always remember that there are two stages on which youth advertising takes place: the physical and the psychological.

Top Ten Youth Brands

I asked everyone I knew, or liked, or walked past at some awards, who was their favourite youth brand, and these are the Top Ten.

1. Apple
"I think Apple is doing a great job. The iPod ad campaign was crafted for the young generation. Great visuals, great music and a very simple, no-nonsense product. Of course, the campaign catapulted the brand from nowhere to market leader. We shouldn't forget that they did not invent the mp3 player. They just simplified it and created iTunes to load music to the iPod. Now iTunes is one of the biggest music shops worldwide. And iPod is a phenomenon." Tolga Büyükdoganay

2. Converse
"I like the legend: Converse. They are just cool. Ever since. A very bold message to a too-settled lifestyle." Goetz Ulmer

3. Stüssy
"I would say a brand like Stüssy. I concede they may have fallen out of favour a bit with their increasing growth, but at the end of the day, I respect brands who have a larger platform to tell their story while remaining cool and credible. I think Stüssy do that quite well. It's no longer about only selling fifty T-shirts, since your ability

to influence or reach people is so limited with those sorts of numbers." Eugene Kan

4. Red Bull
The Red Bull Stratos global stunt was one of the best youth advertising concepts ever. A game-changer, as they say.

5. Nike
It's hard to compete with Nike, and although I don't own any of their shoes, I love the power of the Nike brand – the success of which, incidentally, is all down to an American waffle. Co-founder Bill Bowerman was eating waffles for breakfast one morning, when he realized that a lightweight sole could be made in the same way. He even used his wife's waffle-maker to try the theory out. I learnt that when I went through Nike school before working on the brand back in the day.

6. Vans
Vans were my favourite brand for a long time, as they stayed authentic, but for how long can you keep the accountant from turning you into a "global brand"?

7. H&M
H&M demonstrated how to kill it on the high street without having to sell really shit clothes (leave that to Primark), and keep the standard high by collaborating with desingers such as Karl Lagerfeld, Stella McCartney, Versace, Jimmy Choo, Lanvin and Marni.

8. Dove
Dove defined "keeping it real" by only using real people. I love that and so did a lot of people.

9. Supreme
Dopeness and youth attitude and rebellion personified. End of story.

10. Sony PlayStation
"I have always liked playing PlayStation, because it's the unique brand that has been able to keep perfect connection between me and my son, who is 13 years old. I think this brand will never outdate because its users today are young people and their parents who have been using it since their childhood." Lenilson Lima

Where to Study

I don't think it's something you can just learn, as you have to have the talent to start with. What kind of talent? Well, what I've just spent 352 pages trying to define! But if you think you know what makes a good ad, or you just have original ideas, then perhaps the ad game is for you. There are a few specialist colleges and lots of courses at universities, art schools and technical colleges around the world that offer diplomas and degrees in advertising. I don't think there are any that specialize in youth, but I hope there will be soon. Here's a list of the dedicated ad schools:

AAA School of Advertising
Johannesburg and Cape Town
www.aaaschool.co.za

Berghs School of Communication, Stockholm
www.berghs.se

Chicago Portfolio School, Chicago
www.chicagoportfolio.com

The Creative Circus, Atlanta
www.creativecircus.edu

The Design Factory, Hamburg
www.design-factory.de

Escola Cuca, São Paulo
www.escolacuca.com

Hyper Island, Stockholm, London, Manchester, New York. On- and offline creative courses.
www.hyperisland.com

Miami Ad School, Berlin, Hamburg, Istanbul, Madrid, Mexico City, Miami, Minneapolis, New York, São Paulo and San Francisco
www.miamiadschool.com

Red & Yellow, Cape Town
www.redandyellow.co.za

School of Communication Arts, London
www.schoolcommunicationarts.com

VCU Brandcenter, Richmond, Virginia
www.brandcenter.vcu.edu

Vega School of Brand Leadership, Johannesburg, Durban, Pretoria, and Cape Town
www.vegaschool.com

YoungGuns
Not a college but a good place to get noticed!
www.ygaward.com

D&AD
For the chosen few, their career starts here.
www.dandad.org

Timeline of Incredible Moments

1921. 11 March: "Teen age" appears in the Daily Colonist (Victoria, BC, Canada)
1933. René Lacoste co-founds La Chemise Lacoste
1944. Term "teenager" coined by psychologist G. Stanley Hall
1944. September: Seventeen magazine launches
1945. Eugene Gilbert starts first youth agency: Gil-Bert Teen Age Services. The birth of the youth demographic (16–24 years old)
1962. Bill Bernbach puts the copywriter and art director in the same room
1970. Pregnant man ad
1971. Hip hop begins to emerge
1977. Punk begins
1979. Skating slowly enters the mainstream and becomes a bankable sport
1981. MTV launches...
1982. Internet (Protocol Suite) introduced – a standardized concept of worldwide networking. Oliviero Toscani begins work at Benetton
1984. Stüssy begins to sell clothes. Apple "Big Brother" advert airs just once during the Super Bowl
1992. First smartphone – IMB Simon. Benetton Aids advert
1994. Sony launches PlayStation. First online banner ads on Hotwired site for brands such as Sprint and AT&T. First pay-per-click ads appear on GoTo.com (now part of Yahoo.com)
1995. New Internet architecture with commercial ISPs. Amazon.com begins. First keyword ad "Golf" is launched by Yahoo
1997. First mobile commerce: two vending machines installed in Helsinki, which accept payment via SMS. First mobile ad debuts for Finnish news provider offering free news via SMS. First mobile banking launched, also in Finland by Merita Bank of Finland, also using SMS
1998. Google Search launched
1999. Napster slides onto the radar, for good or for bad
2000. Google AdWords launched
2001. Pop-up ads launched – one of the most hated forms of advertising
2004. Facebook launches
2005. YouTube begins to narrowcast
2006. Twitter goes live, in 140 characters or fewer
2007. May: Google Street View becomes the industry standard. June: iPhone launched. November: Android OS announced...
2010. AKQA launch Nike True City. Droga5's launch for Jay-Z's Decoded becomes a phenomenon

Further Reading and Viewing

Reading
– Heath, Joseph & Andrew Potter, The Rebel Sell: How the Counterculture Became Consumer Culture (Capstone, 2005)
– Hicks, Bill, Love All the People (Constable, 2004)
– Osgerby, Bill, Youth Media (Routledge, 2004)
– Savage, Jon, Teenage: The Creation of Youth 1875–1945 (Pimlico, 2008)
– Underhill, Paco, Why We Buy: The Science of Shopping (Simon & Schuster, 2008)

Viewing
– Art & Copy (Doug Pray, 2009)
– Consuming Kids: The Commercialization of Childhood (Adriana Barbaro & Jeremy Earp, 2008)
– Somers Town (Shane Meadows, 2008)
– The Fine Art of Separating People from Their Money (Hermann Vaske, 1998)
– The Greatest Film Ever Sold (Morgan Spurlock, 2011)

Credits

Text credits

All quotes from interviews conducted by King Adz, 2010–12, apart from:

p. 39: Lee Clow quote lifted from @LeeClowsBeard, Twitter, 8 June 2011

p. 75: Bono quote from Wired magazine issue 15.11, 18 October 2007

p. 75: Andrew Creighton quote from Guardian (Media Section), 22 December 2007

p. 139: Christian Clancy quote from video interview with Al Lindstrom, 6 April 2011

p. 140: Tyler, the Creator, quote from XXL magazine, June edition/website, 7 July 2011

p. 127: Video game figures from The Economist, "All the World's a Game" special report, 10 December 2011

p. 187: Malcolm McLaren quote from The Golden Years of Advertising (Hermann Vaske, 2005)

p. 203: Leo Burnett quote from internal memo, 16 December 1958

p. 205: Federico Lombardi quote from a statement issued by the Vatican, 17 Nov 2011

p. 220: John Lydon quote from The Filth and the Fury (Julien Temple, 2000)

p. 337: George Monbiot quote from the Guardian, 25 October 2011

p. 340: Bill Hicks quote from Love All the People (Constable, 2004)

Image credits

pp. 2, 10, 16, 32, 34–7, 48, 53, 78, 81, 82, 118, 125, 140, 158, 159, 175, 177, 178 (left), 179, 183, 185, 214, 215, 219, 225 (top), 226, 229, 230, 231, 251, 266, 267 (top), 291, 298, 319, 325, 326, 336, 341 King Adz; pp. 8–9 Dasha Yastrebova; p. 11 courtesy of Nike China by W+K Shanghai; p. 15 LICHTFAKTOR; pp. 20, 22 courtesy Stüssy; pp. 23–29 Mother; p. 30 James Day; pp. 38, 40 art by Broken Fingaz; pp. 41–44 KesselsKramer; pp. 45, 49 PS3 courtesy of BBDO Moscow; copywriter: Luis Tauffer; art director: Luis Tauffer; creative directors: Luis Tauffer/Andres Vergara; photographer: Carioca, www.carioca.ro; postproduction: Carioca; pp. 50, 52 Jay-Z Decoded courtesy of Droga5; p. 54 courtesy of Lacoste; p. 57 Levi's courtesy of BBH London; p. 59 Levi's courtesy of The Glue Society; pp. 60, 62 courtesy of Vans; p. 63 art by Roy Poh/A Beautiful Design, Singapore; pp. 65, 66, 68 courtesy of Mother; pp. 69, 71 photos by Diephotodesigner.de; p. 73. stills from films V RAW and Metal on Metal by The Glue Society; pp. 74–77 courtesy of Virtue/VICE; pp. 83, 84 courtesy of AKQA; p. 86 courtesy of MTV Network/George Lois; p. 88 courtesy of Reebok/George Lois; p. 89 courtesy of Tommy Hilfiger/George Lois; pp. 90, 91 courtesy of Esquire/George Lois; p. 92 courtesy of Levi's/Ogilvy Beijing;

p. 95 Cadbury by Rehabstudio; p. 96 (top) courtesy of Diesel; (bottom) courtesy of Britvic/Steve Henry; p. 99 courtesy of Britvic/Steve Henry; pp. 100, 103 courtesy of Diesel; pp. 104, 106 Gummo; p. 107 Rehabstudio; pp. 109, 111 "Don't Tell Ashton"; strategy: Victoria Nyberg & Johan Gerdin; AD: Jonas Åhlen, Felipe Mont & Olle Isaksson; copy: Maja Folgero; PR: Maria Sandberg; project manager: Lina Appelgren; p. 113 courtesy of SHS Teen Clothes; advertising agency: Callegari Berville Grey, Paris; ECD: Andrea Stillacci; creative directors: Giovanni Settesoldi & Luissandro Del Gobbo; art director: Giovanni Settesoldi; copywriter: Luissandro Del Gobbo; illustrator: Claudio Luparelli, Artout; photographer: Riccardo Bagnoli; pp. 119, 122 courtesy of Burger King/Crispin Porter + Bogusky; pp. 123, 124 courtesy of Israel Anti-drug Authority (IADA)/McCann Erikson Tel Aviv; creative director: Nir Refuah; art director: Nir Hersztadt; copywriter: Daniel Barak; photographer: Gooli Cohen; p. 129 (top) courtesy of Fashionary; (bottom) courtesy of Monki; photography by Crista Leonard; p. 130 Crispin Porter + Bogusky Europe; p. 132 courtesy of BLK DNM; pp. 134, 135 DDBeDEZ/Mozambique; p. 136 Martin Barker; pp. 141–51 AKQA; pp. 152–54 Jung von Matt, Sweden; p. 155 JWT Paris; art director, creative director: Giovanni Settesoldi; copywriter, creative director: Luissandro del Gobbo; photographer: Luca Federici; pp. 161, 163 Alex Sainsbury for Barbie x BLEACH; p. 164 photo by James Day; agency: Y&R; creative directors: Shair Zag and Komal Behdi; p. 165 Ren Hang; p. 166 Pancho Tolchinsky; p. 167 Crista Leonard; p. 168 Natasha Bonner; p. 169 Jono; pp. 170–74 Oliviero Toscani; p. 178 (right), 180, 182 Logan Bunting for Waves for Water; p. 186 art by Raul Urias; p. 188 art by Broken Fingaz; p. 189 (top) art by MINGA, (bottom) art by Broken Fingaz; p. 190 LICHTFAKTOR; p. 192 art by Pomme Chan for MTV; p. 194 art by Roy Poh/A Beautiful Design, Singapore; p. 195 art and design by Typejockeys; p. 196 courtesy of Mambo; pp. 198, 199 The Glue Society; pp. 200, 201 SapientNitro; p. 202 art and photo by Zevs; p. 204 (top) art by Ron English; (bottom) art and photo by Eyesaw; p. 206 Ludo; pp. 207, 208 art by Ron English; p. 209 (top) art by Shepard Fairey; (bottom) art by Ron English; p. 210 still from Cousins; pp. 211, 212 courtesy of Truth®; p. 218 (top) Adam Krause; (bottom) Martin Barker; p. 221 Samuel Munyeza; p. 222 A1one; p. 223 Todd Hart; p. 224 (top) Marylin Cayrac; (bottom) Dasha Yastrebova; pp. 225 (bottom), 226 (left), 227, 228 Guy Pitchon; p. 235 courtesy of Nike/Saatchi & Saatchi, São Paulo; iIllustration by Andre Maciel; pp. 237–42 R/GA São Paulo; pp. 243–50 Loducca São Paulo; CCO Guga Ketzer; pp. 254–61 TBWA\Hunt\Lascaris; p. 263 courtesy of Levi's/KingJames;

p. 267 courtesy of Levi's, created by Mat©hboxology; p. 271 Thesis; p. 272 Gloo.co.za; p. 280 AMO Group Bombay; pp. 281–86 Viral Pandya/Out of the Box; p. 287 courtesy of Royal Enfield/W+K Delhi; p. 289 courtesy of BBDO India; p. 292 designers Shivan & Narresh; shot by Parikhit Pal; pp. 293, 294 designer Rimzim Dadu; shot at Wills Lifestyle India Fashion Week; p. 295 courtesy of BBDO India; pp. 302–8 courtesy of Nike China/W+K Shanghai; p. 309 courtesy of Converse; pp. 311, 312 Leong Zhang; p. 313 NeochaEdge; p. 315 art by Honghua/NeochaEdge; pp. 316–18 Hypebeast.com; pp. 323, 324 Art by Dopludo Collective; pp. 327, 329 Boroda Project; p. 330 courtesy of Old Spice/Saatchi & Saatchi Moscow; pp. 332, 334 work by KesselsKramer; p. 342 Poster by Jung von Matt Sweden/Daniel Forero & Leon Phang; pp. 343–5. Photos by Chloe Aftel.

Acknowledgments

Peace+Love to all, especially Wilma, Kaiya, Casius and Zeus. Major respect to all the guest stars...

Index of Guest Stars

Index